Mark Twain and George W. Cable

THE RECORD OF A LITERARY FRIENDSHIP

The Record of a Literary
Friendship

ARLIN TURNER

Mark Twain

G. W. Cable

MICHIGAN STATE UNIVERSITY PRESS
1960

✧ CONTENTS ✧

CONTENTS

✣ PROLOGUE ✣

It has not happened often that the activities of a major author have been recorded day to day by one of his associates. Still less often has the recorder been himself an author of sympathy and perception. Few Dr. Johnsons, that is, have had their James Boswells. Neither George W. Cable nor Mark Twain was in any real sense a Boswell to the other, but for four months in 1884-1885, when each was at the peak of his literary career, they were together constantly as they toured the country sharing the same platforms to read from their books. Letters they wrote during those months report even the smallest incidents in the halls, at the hotels, and on the trains; and with uncommon intimacy the letters reflect the personalities of the two men and the way they saw each other.

Cable sent his wife a letter almost every day he was on the road, some days more than one. These letters fill most of the pages of the present volume. Written in the railway cars, or in their hotel while Mark Twain sang in an adjoining room, or in the retiring room of the hall, as was often the case, while Mark was on the stage drawing waves of laughter and applause from his hearers, Cable's letters reproduce in tone as well as in fact one of the most remarkable joint undertakings in our literary annals. Both members of the reading team wrote now and then to the manager of their tour, Major James B. Pond, and since Pond was a friend to both of them much longer than the duration of the reading tour, their letters to him often contained more than details of travel and local arrangements. The most revealing of these letters are included here also.

In our efforts to fathom Mark Twain's mind and character, we have studied every jot of comment left by those who knew him. Through a touch here and a touch there Cable's letters printed in this volume outline his portrait from an immediacy of observation not equalled in any other extensive comment left by his contemporaries. The portrait was drawn from closer association than perhaps anyone else had with Mark Twain except members of his own household; it reflected abundant understanding and admiration; and it received perspective from the vast differences of temperament and outlook that existed between Cable and his subject. There are also in the letters briefer sketches of Petroleum V. Nasby, Henry Watterson, and others encountered during the tour. Moreover, the letters reveal the writer himself in a way to clear away much of the haze and the apparent conflict from the portrait we have had of him.

The main intention of this book is to print Cable's letters written during the fabulous reading tour with Mark Twain, supplemented by some of the letters, not previously published, which Mark Twain wrote Major Pond at the time; but it has seemed good to include also a few earlier and later letters and other pieces Cable wrote about his friend. Materials already in print, particularly the few letters exchanged between Cable and Mark Twain and Mark's comments on Cable in writing to his wife and to Charles S. Webster, his business partner, have not been included.

The letters of George W. Cable are published with the kind permission of his daughter, Mrs. L. L. C. Biklé. These letters are located now in the Cable Collection at the Tulane University Library. The letters of Mark Twain which are printed here for the first time are published through special arrangements with the Mark Twain Company. Acknowledgement is made to the Henry W. and Albert A. Berg Collection of the New York Public Library, as owner of the physical material, for permission to have made and to use photographic copies of certain letters of Clemens to James B. Pond; to Harper & Brothers for permission to quote excerpts from *Mark Twain's Letters,* edited by A. B. Paine, and from *The Love Letters of Mark Twain,* edited by Dixon Wecter; to Samuel C. Webster for permission to quote from his book, *Mark Twain, Business Man,* published by Little, Brown & Company; and to the American Academy of Arts and Letters for permission to reprint from the *Proceedings* of the Academy Cable's speech at the memorial service for Mark Twain in New York on November 30, 1910.

A GROWING
ACQUAINTANCE

*George W. Cable printed his first criticism of Mark
Twain's works in 1870, and he was one of those who spoke
forty years afterward at the memorial service held in New
York after Mark Twain's death. He was personally acquainted with Mark Twain after 1881, and though he did
not have the long and intimate friendship with Mark
Twain that Joseph Twichell or William Dean Howells
had, he was more constantly in Mark's company during
four months in 1884 and 1885 than either of the others
ever was for an equal span. In letters written to his wife
during these four months he recorded his association
with Mark Twain in delightful and revealing minuteness.*

During 1870 Cable published in the New Orleans
Picayune *a column of miscellaneous comment which he
headed "Drop Shot."[1] He was twenty-six years old, a for-
mer Confederate cavalryman, who since the war had
stolen time from his bookkeeper's desk to write the newspaper pieces which had won him a place as columnist and
reporter. Before the war, when he was fourteen years old,
the death of his father had forced him to leave high
school before graduating, in order to support his mother,
two sisters, and a younger brother. An attack of malarial
fever in 1866 had cut short an apprenticeship in engineer-
ing, but he was no less ambitious afterward than he had*

3

been when he studied mathematics between cavalry forays and when afterward he practised drawing and read American history at night after long hours in a cotton factor's office. Late in 1871 he left the newspaper to become an accountant again, but his year and a half as a columnist had convinced him that his chief interest was literary and also that the materials of literature were rich about him. He was ready, in fact, to undertake serious literary work.

The "Drop Shot" column records the growth of Cable's acquaintance with established literary works and also his awareness of authors just coming on the scene. One of his contemporaries he took up for extended comment was Mark Twain. In his column of July 17, 1870, he compared Mark Twain with Josh Billings, a humorist in epigrams whose real name was Henry Wheeler Shaw:

Mark Twain is a man of the living to-day. With so much force of mind and energy of pen, with such practical sympathy with the themes and actions of the present, that his jesting betrays something of the tradesman's (for the world is one big tradesman now) restraint and method, and his humor must run a long way before it makes a sumersault. There is almost too much of the Morgan horse in his build to make frolicking easy and natural. If you would laugh at Mark you must first hear him through; but good old Josh is fun from first to last, and was born with the art of being wise and silly in a breath. Mark moves always with the laughing point of view as a goal, but Josh carries a thousand laughs with him, loaded like a Santa Claus.

It may be that the superior weight of mind is Mark Twain's, for his descriptions of Oriental scenery that are without humor are productions of rare beauty, and some of his humorous inventions show a power of satire that will compare favorably with writers of higher fame. They make a mistake to call his Frog story his masterpiece, and fail to apprehend the true genius of the man. We recall nothing that so plainly shows at the best what Mark Twain is as the "Beef Contract." There is there an actual tangible something to make war against, and the sword of sarcasm flashes like fire as it falls upon the trickeries of the Government. He is too practical to be a Quixote, and only Josh Billings can be a Sancho Panza.

In point of moral tone, "sly old J. B." is certainly in advance, for while all that can be said of Mark Twain is that he writes little that has harm in it, his fellow joker is as full of goodness as a bunch of berries. His quaint saws and misspelt proverbs are better than Poor Richard.

While we have that misspelling in hand, let me say there is very little credit in it. However, others try and fail, and people will laugh as long as Josh Billings does it, though there's no more real wit in it than in a grimace; yet it is the vehicle of that quality of playfulness so necessary to a humorist: and this indeed is what is most notably lacking in Mark Twain.

If we had to part with one of them, it would not be easy to choose. As for us give us Josh Billings. Mark spins a good yarn, but Josh is such a blessed old fool.

These paragraphs show that Cable knew Mark Twain's two published volumes, The Celebrated Jumping Frog of Calaveras County and Other Sketches *(1867) and* The Innocents Abroad *(1869); but he would as a matter of*

*course have known also Mark's sketches which passed
from one newspaper to another over the nation. It was in
keeping with Cable's bent for moral teaching that he
valued Mark Twain as a satirist and a reformer, just as
he valued Josh Billings still higher because he joined wit
and wisdom in every sentence.*

*When Mark Twain and Cable first met in 1881, both
were in full career as authors. Mark Twain had published
a burlesque autobiography in 1871,* Roughing It *in 1872
and* The Gilded Age *a year later in collaboration with
Charles Dudley Warner. In* Tom Sawyer *after three more
years he had begun the re-creation of his Missouri boyhood which was to be his major achievement. Cable had
published seven stories in* Scribner's Monthly *beginning
in 1873 and had collected them into* Old Creole Days *in
1879. Then his first novel,* The Grandissimes *(1880),
was published serially and as a volume. With these two
books he had established Creole New Orleans as his particular fictional realm. He was compared often with
Hawthorne, Alphonse Daudet, and Victor Hugo, and still
better work was expected of him.*

*While in the East, Cable went to Hartford on June 11,
1881, to visit the Bartletts, relatives of his wife. Four
days later he wrote home:*

I went to see Charles Dudley Warner. Found him, his
brother George & Mrs. George Warner. It is hard to
realize now that I have known these kind, gentle, hearty
friends only four days. They telegraphed at once to Mr.
Clemens (Mark Twain) to come up—from somewhere
beyond New Haven. On Monday they came—taking the
first train that started after their rec't of telegram. . . .

Both Mr. & Mrs. Clemens came, Mrs. Clemens "inviting herself," as she said. The Warners sent out in every direction to intercept us (George Warner & I) & finally succeeded.

And so I met Mark Twain. We all lunched together & "Mark" & Mr. Warner were ever so funny. But soon the Clemenses had to bid us good-bye & return to the cars & to New Haven. I will tell you all about it some day, from the hearty meeting to the pleasant but regretful parting. . . . My visit to Hartford was a perfect ovation.[2]

Before the end of the year Cable resigned his business affiliations to rely on his "grey goose pen," he said, "for both offense and defense." It was as an author full-time, then, that he entertained Mark Twain in New Orleans in April of the next year. Mark had come to visit the Mississippi River, intending to put his observations into chapters to supplement the articles he had published in the Atlantic Monthly *of 1875 under the title "Old Times on the Mississippi." Thus he filled out a book, which appeared in 1883 as* Life on the Mississippi. *He reached New Orleans on April 28, 1882, accompanied by a stenographer and his friend James R. Osgood, the Boston publisher. During a visit of ten days in the city he was almost constantly with Cable, whom he called in* Life on the Mississippi *"the South's finest literary genius," and the "only master in the writing of French dialects that the country has produced." He made it clear also how much he valued Cable as a cicerone, "to see . . . and describe and explain and illuminate" the old French city as they drove through its narrow streets, and to give them "a vivid*

sense *as of unseen or dimly seen things—vivid, and yet
fitful and darkling.*"³

*On Monday afternoon in Cable's study, after Joel
Chandler Harris had come from Atlanta to join them
on Sunday, Cable and Mark Twain read each from his
own books, and they read also from Uncle Remus, for
Harris would not read even to gratify the children who
were present.⁴ On other occasions also there was reading
and singing—at the home of Cable's friend James B.
Guthrie on Monday night, for example, and at John's
Restaurant on Tuesday night when E. A. Burke, manager
of the New Orleans* Times-Democrat, *entertained them.
The paper reported that Mark Twain was especially
pleased with Cable's singing of the Creole dialect songs.*

*Mark Twain's own habits invited others to join in the
teasing and practical joking; and the twinkle habitually
in Cable's eye bespoke a love of fun no less pervasive
though more disciplined than Mark Twain's. As Mark
Twain boarded the steamer commanded by his old men-
tor in the pilot house, Horace E. Bixby, to begin his trip
back up the river on May 6, a young man just being introduced said to him: "I have read all of your writings
Mr. Twain, but I think I like the Heathen Chinee the
best of them all." Mark Twain's friends knew what dis-
taste he had come to have for Bret Harte and it was a
favorite joke of theirs to call him the author of this or
some other of Harte's works. The episode was recounted
in the* Times-Democrat *of the next morning, and there
seems little doubt that Cable was responsible for having
it reported, if indeed he did not manage to have the incident staged—especially in view of the fact that he retold
it twenty-three years later when he rose to speak at*

Mark Twain's seventieth birthday party in New York and that he alluded to it again when he spoke at the memorial service after Mark Twain's death.[5]

Following this visit in New Orleans, Mark Twain and Cable corresponded with some regularity and sought ways to befriend each other.[6] Mark's schemes to rob the public, such as often were born in the Colonel Sellers side of his brain, began to include his friend in New Orleans. One of his schemes would bring William Dean Howells, Thomas Bailey Aldrich, Joel Chandler Harris, Cable, and himself together in a "menagerie" for a joint reading tour of the country. Cable regretted to see the proposal abandoned, for he was thinking of the platform as a means of supplementing his literary income. On his next trip east late in 1882 Cable visited Hartford, in answer to Mark Twain's urging, and together they went to Boston for the evening which Mark described in the often-quoted letter he wrote on November 4 to Howells, then on his way to Italy:

Cable has been here, creating worshipers on all hands. He is a marvelous talker on a deep subject. I do not see how even Spencer could unwind a thought more smoothly or orderly, and do it in a cleaner, clearer, crisper English. He astounded Twichell with his faculty. You know when it comes down to moral honesty, limpid innocence, and utterly blemishless piety, the Apostles were mere policemen to Cable; so with this in mind you must imagine him at a midnight dinner in Boston the other night, where we gathered around the board of the Summerset Club; Osgood, full, Boyle O'Reilly, full, Fairchild responsively loaded, and Aldrich and myself possessing the floor and properly fortified. Cable told Mrs. Clemens when we returned here, that he seemed to have been entertaining himself with horses, and had a dreamy idea that he must have gone to Boston in a cattle-car. It was a very large time. He called it an orgy. And no doubt it was, viewed from his standpoint.[7]

Roswell Smith, president of the Century Company and Cable's warmest friend among his publishers in New York, had undertaken to see him started on the lecture platform and had enlisted others to help. In October, 1882, Richard Watson Gilder, editor of the Century Mag-*azine, took Cable to Baltimore, where he met Daniel Coit Gilman, president of Johns Hopkins University, and made arrangements to deliver six lectures the following March. Then while Cable was in Baltimore giving the lectures, Roswell Smith took the matter up again, and it was decided that Cable should make an appearance in Hartford, where Mark Twain and Charles Dudley Warner and his brother George agreed to do the managing. It was with barely restrained delight that Cable accepted the invitation to Hartford and assured Mark Twain, in answer to his re-quest, that he would make no further plans for readings until they met.*

The Hartford Daily Courant *of March 27 printed the letter which had been sent Cable on the fifteenth inviting him "in behalf of the many admirers of your writings in this city, and in furtherance of a general desire to hear you in public," to lecture in Hartford. The letter was signed by Clemens, Charles Dudley Warner, General Joseph R. Hawley, Joseph H. Twichell, and a dozen others. Along with it was printed Cable's acceptance, in which he set April 4 as the date and "Creole Women" as his subject. Meanwhile Cable had added to his six scheduled lectures in Baltimore a seventh appearance, by request, in which he read from his own works. Of this reading he wrote Mark Twain on March 20: "The Hall was simply cramfull & the audience in almost continual laughter. It's touchingly gratifying to hear them laugh & applaud where nothing funny is intended." On the same day he wrote his wife:*

My reading was a *great* success. The hall was absolutely packed & the doors shut with others outside unable to enter. Even the little side-room that opens upon the platform & by which the lecturer steps in upon it was crowded with standing ladies and gentlemen. Except in Bras-Coupé, where the hush that followed the story of his death was followed by applause, the house was in almost incessant laughter. When as Colossus I turned about suddenly & said to Pres/t Gilman—"ain't dat so, boss," the house roared & applauded to the echo. All through I could hear Pres/t Gilman's hearty "ha, ha!" & when I sat down at the close of their severe 60 minute limit he said, "that's nothing, go on," & I went on, & read Joseph's visit to the Nancanou ladies.[8]

The Baltimore papers had praised the six lectures as equaling if not surpassing earlier lectures by James Russell Lowell and Sidney Lanier, and they had especially commended the reading, the Baltimore American *saying on March 20, "Since the days when Charles Dickens read his own droll stories, it is doubtful whether any novelist has appeared before an American audience so*

*well prepared to interpret his own writings as Mr. Cable."
Gilman had written for the* Critic *of March 24⁹ a glowing
report of Cable's Johns Hopkins lectures and especially
the final reading. When they saw these testimonials,
Clemens and Warner proposed that the reading be repeated at Hartford, as the surest way of achieving favor-
able publicity for Cable's platform work. He readily
acceded, though he kept the title "Creole Women" and
planned to string the selections together with comment
on the Creoles of the past and the present.*

*After stopping in New York and on March 26 address-
ing the Congregational Club on prison reform, and after
visiting in New Haven, where he went with introductions
Gilman had given him, he reached Hartford on April 2.
Letters to his wife recount his visit there.*

Hartford, Apl 2, 1883.

I arrived here at noon today.[10] Am writing at Charles
Warner's table in a bay window looking upon the grey,
wintry landscape with its patches of reluctantly melting
snow.

Charles D. Warner met me at the door just leaving
for New York. He will be back to my lecture on Wednesday. His wife is at the piano practicing for a little afternoon musicale appointed for tomorrow at this house.

I have been over to see Clemens. Found him sick or
nearly so, lying down at least with a cold. He promises
to be up tonight, when some of us expect to attend the
meeting of the Monday club. Mr. Twichell came in while
I was there, looking for me. All ask kindly after you. Mrs.
George Warner is as sweet [as] ever. She had me get your
own & the children's pictures out as soon as I had lunched

after arrival. George Warner has not yet come in from business.

A little while ago a Miss Perkins called to ask me to appear before the Hartford Sat'y Morn'g Club (of young ladies) which meets on Thursday this time in order to have me there. I fixed Thursday morning & will read before them, I think, from Posson Jone'.

It was delightful, the meeting with my friends & the greeting I rec'd. As soon as I have dined I must go out & see the Bartletts.

Mrs. Clemens is sick abed with quinzy, but out of all danger & today greatly improved. . . .

Hartford, Conn.
Ap'l 3, 1883.

Nothing to add to yesterday's letter. Only to let you know all goes well. Dear old Mark Twain sends kindest word to all of you, beginning, of course, with Nellie.[11] His wife is not materially better this morning.

We have a beautiful day today. I ventured over to M. T.'s house without my overcoat & felt comfortable; but on starting away from his house he cried out at the idea of no overcoat.

I said "the air is full of a soft, warm glow."

"Soft warm glow! It's full of the devil!—the devil of pneumonia! That's what it's full of!" And so I had to wear one of his overcoats back to Warner's.

Here's another characteristic speech. "Yes, sir, my poor wife must get sick, & have a pulse that ran up to— 150 in the shade!"

He began to d—n Roswell Smith (whom he likes very well, I believe). I said I don't allow my friends to abuse each other. "Yes, that's all right; I know that. That's the reason I forbear as I do. You see how mild my abuse is compared to what it would be if you were not here."

He strode up & down the room holding his headachy forehead & brandishing his arms, scolding over the various miscarriages of our schemes concerning the reading.

I said "I didn't come over here to torment you before your time." He answered—

"O you're not tormenting me; only give me room to swear!" But he did not swear—much.

I went last evening to see the Bartletts. . . .

The musicale was beautiful. . . . Mrs. Warner one of the very best pianists I *ever* heard. Mary Bartlett played. . . .

All the ladies were in raptures over the children's pictures and—thine, thou dear girl!

'Twas not I, but Mrs. Warner who exhibited them.

Well, I must close. Mrs. Cha/s Dudley Warner & a gentleman friend are playing a beautiful duet. Mrs. George Warner sends love. . . .

Tomorrow the reading.

Thursday the Monday Club gives me a lunch. . . .

For several days before the reading the publicity was steady in the Hartford papers. Besides routine announcements there were long quotations from the Baltimore papers praising Cable's performances there, and there were pieces signed by Mark Twain, such as the following: "Mr. Cable is a reader and speaker whose matter is of the finest quality and whose arts of delivery are of distinguished excellence. It seems well to state this, in order that the public may know that Mr. Cable has something more to offer his audience, as an attraction, than his cele-

brated person alone." In a note which the Hartford
Courant *quoted on April 2 from the Hartford* Times *a
call was made to local pride: "It would be a reflection
upon the literary taste of the city to suppose that there
are not here enough admirers of Mr. Cable's novels to
fill Unity Hall with an appreciative audience. It is certain
that a rare treat will be offered on that occasion by that
brilliant young southern author."*

*In Unity Hall on April 4 Cable stood before an audience,
in the words of the* Courant *reporter of the next day,
"such as rarely assembles to greet the greatest favorite
on the lecture platform." He first described lower Louisiana and New Orleans—houses, gardens, fields, and people.
Then he read from* Old Creole Days *and* The Grandissimes. *The* Courant *said:*

His reading is so absolutely simple that we hesitate to
apply the word dramatic to it, and yet the effect was
dramatic, as the intense interest with which his sketch-
ing was followed by the audience attested. We saw as we
had hardly seen in reading his writings how exceedingly
subtle is his method, how delicate and refined is his color
and drawing. . . . In the dialogues, especially in the
Creole dialect, which is so musical on his lips, he held
his audience almost breathless under the spell he wove
so quietly and without apparent effort. . . . The entertainment was in its character so simple and unostentatious
that it was not until the reader had finished that the
audience began to realize the delicate creation, the charming unfamiliar picture that the author had conjured out
of the air. . . .

Cable kept up his reports home:

Hartford, April 5, 1883.

I never wanted to lay my tired head in your hands more than I do this morning. The reading here is done. It was a decided success and was delivered to a full house. Osgood & Waring & Gilder, & Roswell Smith & Hutton and Warner were there,[12] (all but R/Smith being on the platform) & Mark Twain introduced me. He was immensely funny. However, I suppose you'll see all this in the papers.

After the lecture Mark gave us (the above party) a supper at the Hartford Clubhouse. Rev. Joe. Twichell was there & there was abundance of innocent fun. There were a hundred good things said that I suppose I'll never recall.

This morning I must read to the Saturday-Morning Club (of young ladies) & at 1 P. M. go to the lunch given me by the Monday Club. . . .

The Courant *of the next day reported Mark Twain as introducing Cable by saying that as a rule the introducer is less known than the one introduced, and hence the necessity to have the introducer introduced. But in view of those who had come from distant parts and were seated on the platform, he said, the customary practice must be abandoned and the speaker must proceed without an introduction.*

Hartford, April 5, 1883.

. . . In the letter w'h I wrote you this morning you must have discerned some dejection of spirit & wondered what it meant if last night's reading was a success. Well, it was this: the success was not the *kind* that one must have in order to make such a reputation that people will fill a hall whenever & wherever he is announced to appear.

Poor, dear old Mark Twain! I could see that his wide experience recognized the fact & that he was not satisfied. The hall was full. There were some seats in the gallery not occupied but on the other hand there were more persons standing than would have filled all those vacant seats. And I felt sore to think that if that same entertainment were repeated not *all* those people would have return'd.

So enough of last night. This morning I went to the Saturday-Morning Club meeting at the residence of Mr. Cha/s Perkins and read them Posson Jone'. There were many invited guests. Gilder was among them. Mark Twain had offered last night as we were coming home in the carriage, to introduce me with a short speech. I didn't accept the offer. I thought his huge horse fun of last night had been one of the causes of my partial short-coming; it had seemed to throw me out of key. I know, *now,* it wasn't that. But this morning I asked him, the moment we met, to do as he had offered. I knew he would do something good & guessed that he had some special thought. So it was. He represented me as an im-poster and charlatan—oh pshaw! If I try to tell it I shall only make it seem stupid, whereas it was royally funny and kind & affectionate by innuendo.

"He will now read you one of his *stories* not to call them by any harder name. But if any of you are offended at his pernicious utterances you have only to rise in your place & I'll stop him at once."

The reading was the greatest success I have ever made in my life. The whole company was completely enraptured.

They said that in the 5 years of their corporate existence they had never had such an entertainment. Clemens told me as we went away, walking along alone, that he had seen Bayard Taylor, Howells, Henry James, Jr., Bret Harte, & others before that club, but never before had he seen them so worked upon & drawn out.—"Why they *forgot* themselves, that's what they did!"

He was absolutely happy. Gilder was in glee. "You must read that in Madison Square Theatre," he cried the moment I was done. The ladies did not know how to be done thanking me. Some took my hand in both their own. Within a half hour past I have received a lovely loose bouquet . . . with the compliments of the club.

From the club we took a carriage—it seems as if Clemens' chief end in life is to spend hack-hire—and went to the lunch in my honor at the Hartford Club house by members of the Monday Evening Club. Here's the table [plan showing the people placed]. . . .

It was the maddest, merriest three hours—the wittiest uproar that *ever* I heard in my life. It beat the Boston dinner of last fall and was without the grossness which hurt my ear there.[13]

"Well," cried Mark Twain at last when they were all weary with laughing, drawing a sigh, "we might as well leave here; I can't think of anything else to say—that is, anything that's decent." It was a slam at me, of course. So we dispersed. I think it—

—The bell for Tea—

Morning, 6th Apl, 1883.

I forget what I was going to say. I went with the Bartletts to church. Heard a few tolerably good remarks from Dr. Parker & then some of the rambling stuff from a rev'd friend of his. Coming back stopped by Mark Twain's a moment to hand him a letter from Mary Bartlett. I dropped the statement that Dr. Parker made a few cursory remarks.

"What! not right there in church?" he asked with a look of grave astonishment.

I regarded him with loathing pity.

"My conscience, Clemens, have you sunk to that?"— He drew up his poor legs into the arm chair & groveled in it—"Yes"—(abjectly)—"Yes, I got down at last to puns! You may take that one to Charlie Warner with my love." I complained that I had seen so many handle that one that I didn't know whether it was his or whose.

"—That's *so*. It's a *beau*tiful antique."

But why should I fill my letters with this puerile horse fun. It sounds good enough when it's first said, & I enjoy it greatly. . . .

This evening I read for the Warners to as many friends as they can gather into their rather small rooms. Tomorrow go down to Newport, dine with the Warings, meet "Susan Coolidge"[14] (She is *larger* than Co/l Waring), spend Sunday in Newport & go Monday morning to New York.

Last night Clemens handed me over the bills & a/c's of the lecture with Major Kinney's[15] little check for a bal/ce of a/c. The lecture nets me $125. Light is breaking, sweetheart. . . .

*In his enthusiasm at hearing Cable read "Posson Jone'"
Gilder perhaps forgot for the moment that as editor of*
Scribner's Monthly *he had rejected that story. Published
in* Appletons' Journal, *April 1, 1876, it was the only one
of Cable's early stories that did not appear first in* Scribner's.

Hartford, April 7, 1883.

I am about to go to Newport. It is a rainy morning. Mr.
Clemens' carriage will be along in a few minutes & I shall
be taken to the depot.

The dear Warners! I hate to say goodbye to them. I
don't think you ever could imagine the depth of eager
solicitude that Chas. D. W. & Clemens have shown for
me. Major Kinney attended to all the details of preparation for the lecture & was so tired after it that he couldn't
stay to the club-room supper. All the compensation I or
Clemens could make him take was a set of my works.

Last night I read to the Warners' guests. There were
55 of them. Clemens was absent—staid away with his
poor sick wife to let the others of the household come.
Everybody seemed quite carried away by the reading.

I leave here under the delightful assurance that my dear
friends part with me perfectly convinced that my future
is open to me & that great success is in store. May God's
cause be advanced thereby and grace be given His servant
to promote His glory both within himself & throughout the
world. . . .

*Since the age of fourteen Cable had been the chief
support of his mother. In almost every letter he wrote
her while he was in the army and during the uncertain*

*years afterward, he told her he expected better times
would come and her lot would be easier. Now he could tell
her hopefully of the "green and roseate spring" he saw
ahead.*

April 7, 1883.

I am on a railway train between Hartford & Newport. . . .

. . . My visit to Hartford has been full of pleasure & of
profit. A new future appears to be opening before me. To
us the brown winter of the past seems just ready to give
birth to a green & roseate spring, and if it be so I rejoice
that you have been spared to share it.

I left Hartford without being able to see Mrs. Clemens.
She is slowly & tediously improving. . . .

I scored another emphatic success last evening in a
reading before a small drawing-room audience of 55
persons at Mr. Warner's house. Charles Dudley Warner
was delighted with it. He kept away from me until I
had heard all the adulation of the 55, & when all the
house was abed but he & I, said "now let's come down to
business." The only criticism he had was a warning to
speak loud & slow enough when I get into a large hall.
All the rest was discussion of my literary method, which
he puts above all other American fictionists. . . .[16]

*In 1880 George E. Waring had gone to New Orleans to
collect social statistics for publication with the United
States census and had appointed Cable his assistant. Since
that time he had been Cable's staunch booster among the
publishers of his acquaintance.*

21

Newport
Apl 8, 1883.
I sit at Co/l Waring's desk in his study. . . . After dinner others were sent for on my replying affirmatively to the Warings' request that I would read to a small company. . . . Mark Twain had written an enthusiastic letter to Co/l Waring about my rendering of Posson Jone' & so they wanted that. I gave it. They expressed great delight. . . .

Before going to Hartford, Cable had contracted to read in the Madison Square Theatre in New York, and though his performance there on April 23 left much to be desired, chiefly because, as the New York World *said the next day, his voice was not adequate for the hall and the stories he undertook to read, he returned to New Orleans nevertheless hopeful for a future on the stage. A commencement address at the University of Louisiana (later Tulane University) on June 15[17] and an address on prison reform before the National Conference of Charities and Correction at Louisville on September 26[18] gave him further experience, and he went directly from Louisville to New York, where he settled down to take voice lessons while he booked engagements for reading in the coming season. His first appearance was to be at Springfield, Massachusetts, on November 21, and on the morning of that day he wrote his wife from Hartford.*

Hartford, Nov/r 21st 1883.
Here I am in Mark Twain's house again. This time Mrs. Clemens is well & beautiful & all is brightness &

happiness. All the Warners are well & send love. So are the Bartletts.

Went with Clemens & the Warners to a reception last night & saw many people. Talked my head off; but don't worry, there wasn't anything in it.

Off by & by for Springfield. Pardon these hasty scrawls.

I read last night to Mark T, his sweet wife, her mother, & Clara and her sister. They were pleased. . . .

Following the Springfield appearance, Cable went to Boston to read in the new Chickering Hall on November 26 and 28 and December 4. There he received more flattering attention than ever before. William Dean Howells, Oliver Wendell Holmes, and others endorsed him in the papers; Charles Fairchild, J. R. Osgood, and Howells entertained him. John Greenleaf Whittier called at his room and said, "I've read every line thee ever wrote, and I knew thee would be a great writer as soon as I saw thy first productions."[19] All literary and social Boston, in fact, seemed to be showering him with honors. One reporter said that Matthew Arnold and Henry Irving, both of whom had appeared there recently, had neither been accorded such unreserved acclaim.[20] To his retiring room after a reading would come a procession of literary people —Francis Parkman, J. T. Trowbridge, T. W. Higginson, Elizabeth Stuart Phelps, and Horace E. Scudder on one evening—smearing him over with flattering speeches, he wrote his wife on December 14, "but it brushes off when it is dry—at least I hope it does." The Springfield Republican *could account for Boston's idolatry of Cable only by saying that he had invented a new pleasure.*

At first the Boston newspapers were generous but re-

---

served in their reports; by December 5, however, they had abandoned all reserve. The Evening Transcript said on that day that Cable's work could be compared only with Hawthorne's; for a comparison with his acting, it continued, "we should be obliged to go back to the actors of the Shakespearian era . . . , and the musical quality of his ringing voice is in perfect accord with this mental flexibility." To the three readings originally scheduled for Boston Cable added two more, and he crowded appearances in five other cities into the days before Christmas. On December 12 he reported to Major Pond: "I am just in from a successful reading at Cambridge. Audience tried to call me back a second time, after first encore. Of course it was very pleasant to me. Full house. At matinée here yesterday, not an empty standing room, much less a seat. Audience delighted. Give another matinée here on Friday. Half the house sold this morning in 30 minutes." "Every dog has his day, even the stump-tailed ones," he had written his wife on December 5. "This is mine. I'm the fashion of the moment." Three days later he had told of seeing Roswell Smith in New York: "He said, 'Well, it has come at last. Remember, we prayed to the Lord for this & He has given it to us'—meaning the success which is now pouring in upon me like a flood."

At the middle of December Cable signed a contract engaging Major James B. Pond to manage his readings. Though most programs by that time had been filled for the season, Pond was able to book readings in the Eastern and Midwestern cities from the middle of January to late spring. From New York Cable wrote his wife on January 25: "Mark Twain is here in the Everett. Had me engage a room for him as Mr. James P. Jones & goes by that

name here. *I had him & Yung Wing²¹ to breakfast with
me this morning—jolly time. We all three leave on the
N. Haven road this evening, they for Hartford, I for N.
Haven."* On January 26 he read at Hartford, and the
following morning he awoke at Mark Twain's house suffer-
ing from what was diagnosed as neuralgia of the lower jaw,
but what after he was well and gone proved to be mumps,
it seems, for his nurse and the Clemens children came
down with the mumps. Mark Twain, apparently more dis-
turbed than anyone else, notified Cable's friends, and he
or his wife or one of the Warners sent letters to New
Orleans regularly until February 8, when Cable could sit
up part of each day and write for himself. His stay in
Hartford is amply recorded in those letters.

Mark Twain's House
Monday Hartford. Jan. 28th, '84.

Don't laugh at me, Mrs. George Warner is my amanuensis for today, as a slight indiscretion has given me a
savage little attack of neuralgia in that part of my face
that I make my living by, in short, my lower jaw—the
part that wags, and the doctor, in order to make short
work of it, has ordered me to keep my bed for twenty four
hours. That's all. . . .

Our dear friends in Hartford are, without exception,
well. Both the Messrs. Warner are away. . . .

Now a word, dear Mrs. Cable, on my own account. Do
not feel troubled—Your husband is really doing well, and
will not be detained here long—and Mrs. Clemens promises to dismiss him in good condition.

We all enjoy so much seeing him again, and having
another rich evening from him. The lovely cream-white

roses, which the Young Ladies of the Sat. Morning Club gave him, he intended to send at once to you—not hoping they could reach you in any freshness, alas! I will take them out of the fountain in the conservatory—where I wish you could see them—and start them on their long journey.

I am delighted to hear that you are so well—and wish I could see that dear little new girlie you have to rejoice in. I hope you can come northward again before very long. Mrs. Clemens joins with me in love to you. We all want so much to see you here.

Sincerely yours
Lilly G. Warner

Hartford. Tuesday A. M.
Jan. 29th, 1884.

Here we are again. Mrs. Warner and you and I—all strictly confidential. I expect to be up some time today, and hope to be on the platform tomorrow night. If you could see how I am taken care of, I am afraid you would consider it a great waste of kindness. (The amanuensis must always write precisely what is dictated no matter how unreasonable! L. W.) I've nothing special to say today, and I am saving my strength, doing all I can to get on my feet at the earliest moment. . . .

Yours forever.

Witness my hand & seal this 29th day of Jan'y, 1884.

G. W. Cable.

Will you be so kind, dear Mrs. Cable, as to send me the two photogs. of Mrs. Clemens which I sent for you to see, by your husband last spring, as I find there are no more to be had.

Mr. Cable seems to be much better today—but we all are anxious to have him get quite well before he starts off again.

I put so much wrapping about the roses that I have a half hope they will reach you a little fresh after all— and am really anxious to know if such a thing is possible after so long a travel. ...

Yours, sincerely, L. G. Warner

Hartford Jan 30th, 1884

I might address your letters dear Madame & pretend to my friends that I have a very exalted respect for you, but the flippancy that takes irresistible hold upon me, would betray me before I could turn the page.

I have not thought best to telegraph to you as a telegram itself being so infrequent a thing at our house would give you more dread than comfort. (Excuse me, I just stopped to take five quinine pills.)

Now to come to the subject. I didn't sit up yesterday, but I may easily do so this afternoon. I have had a hard & ugly fight while it lasted, with neuralgia in the jaw. You can tell little Mary that it would have done her heart good, if her heart wasn't so good already, to see how father had to keep his mouth shut when he didn't want to.

In a day or two I shall be in New York and in the old highway robbery business. ... We have new ties now binding us to our Hartford friends. ... Yours forever

George

I forgot to say that it is Mrs. Clemens today who is so kind as to be the medium of communication between us. Dear Mrs. Cable

You need have no anxiety as regards Mr. Cable. I know it is useless to say that, still he is doing well, and will I think be about in a day or two.

With sympathy

Yours

Olivia L. Clemens

Mark Twain wired Cable's wife on January 30, "Your husband will be out of bed by tomorrow." The Clemens children were Susy, Clara, and Jean, aged eleven, nine, and three.

Hartford Jan 31st, 1884

I must still write to you one more letter by dictation, my head is full of quinine, and I find it very hard to think. Don't let me give you the idea that some grave matter has laid me up, and that you ought to be with me—my illness is over, and I would be feeling very nice today, but for the effects, first of opiates and now of quinine. . . .

I have every want gratified here and every freak of a sick man's mind, I have even the pleasure of knowing that I am not the same burden on the household here that I might be in less favored latitudes, or in plainer words I have a regular trained nurse from the training school, who does everything with the greatest perfection.

I have enjoyed Mr. Clemens' company today not a little. When I come home I will try to repeat to you some of the funny stories he tells the little Jean. Jean has a magnificent mental digestion, she must have a tiger in every story; and no tiger seems to her to be really worth the money unless he's in a jungle. Imagine Walter[22] telling stories to Jean and illustrating them as he talked.

The Warner ladies have been in to see me, how beautiful upon the mountains are the feet of them. . . .

But Cable's recovery was slow. In letters already published[23] Olivia sent reports to New Orleans on February 1, 6, and 7; Lilly G. Warner on the second. Letters in Cable's own hand began on the eighth. Meanwhile scheduled readings must be cancelled.

Hartford, Feb 8, 1884.

It is night & I am in bed; so my lines must be few; but I write tonight because I think I shall get this into an earlier mail than I could a letter written tomorrow morning.

I have sat up much today, & hope to move about the house tomorrow beyond the limits of my room. I cannot get away from here yet for two or three days more. Major Pond tells me my business is not hurt—only delayed. . . .

Hartford, Feb 9, 1884.

I am up & out of my sick room. I have a sweet letter from you this morning urging me to give exact information as to my sickness.

I have had a neuralgic-intermittent fever. I have never been in danger & hope now to be on the platform again in a few days. . . .

. . . You can't imagine what good care has been taken of me. It is only just now, for the first time in nearly 2 weeks that I have fed myself, though I have been eating all the time.

I never imagined such an amount of comfort & con-

solation possible to be enjoyed by an invalid & con-
valescent. . . .

Hartford, Feb'y 10, 1884.

I have been up today nearly all day. The afternoon is
wearing along and I am feeling well & only a little weak.

I have seen some friends today who dropped in from
church, telling what a fine sermon Mr. Twichell had just
preached. First, Mrs. Chas Dudley Warner & then Mr.
George Warner. Mrs. Clemens, too, came into my room
& Dr. Davis, my physician. . . .

After my dinner I returned to the library & had a long
chat with Mark Twain. Now he has gone out with the
children for a walk, Mrs. Clemens is upstairs, my nurse
lies fast asleep on the lounge just beside me, & all is still.
I look out upon the snowy prospect & think of home.

Clemens has finished the play he was writing when I
fell ill and has commenced a new work.[24] He is in splen-
did working trim. I seem to have made great way in the
hearts of these dear good people. Clemens, specially,
seems to warm to me more & more.

Well, I mustn't tire myself. In fact there seems to be
always some reason why I should take a selfish attitude
of ease or indulgence. . . .

Hartford, Feb 11, 1884.

. . . The doctor promises me much more liberty after
today. I shall soon be out & well unless I have a setback—
which I am guarding against with all my might. . . .

Hartford, Feb 12, '84.

I am so much better that I have come up Mark's great
hallstair (4 short flights) and am in his study, sitting

———

by his west window. Time is short & dinner will soon be called & I must go to dinner with the family. My nurse is dismissed.

Goodbye, sweet. I have just answered a telegram from Pond telling him I am all right for the 19th for Phila. . . .

Hartford, Feb 13, 1884.

I do not write letters these days worthy to be called such, for I am letting myself alone to get strong as fast as my nature will let me.

I wish I could write long today, for I have enjoyed the day extremely. From the breakfast table Clemens & I went into the drawing-room. He was complaining that he had overworked during the last few days & was tempted to take a half holiday. We sat down together & fell a-chatting. Time passed & we continued talking. He finished his pipe & as we went on each seemed to kindle the other's mind & so we kept up our converse. By & by we were both on our feet, he walking up & down the drawing-room & I back & forth across it. Our talk was generally earnest—about our great Century & the vast advantages of living in it—the glory & beauty of it, etc., etc.

Only when we were talking of publishers [did] Mark get ferocious & funny.

"Oh!" he groaned with longing, in contemplation of discomfiting some fellows who he thinks have cheated him in copyright, "if it could be, I could lie in my grave with my martial cloak around me & kick my monument over & laugh & laugh!"

He went to the piano & sang a German song—one that Longfellow has translated—

"O, hemlock tree, O hemlock tree,
  How faithful are thy branches."[25]

I felt in voice & sang a tenor part not trying to use the words. Then back to our talk and out to the library where Mark proposed a little literary scheme for him & I & 3 or 4 others; & when Mrs. Clemens came in at 1 P. M. we were still talking.

Part of the time—I forgot to say—was spent in consulting Audubon to identify a strange & beautiful bird that we had seen at breakfast time from the window of the library.

Goodbye, sweetheart. Mrs. Clemens is reading aloud to Mark & the children. Howard Pyle's beautiful new version of Robin Hood.[26] Mark enjoys it hugely; they have come to the death of Robin & will soon be at the end.

Goodbye. As soon as the weather clears up, now, I shall be off for New York. . . .

The literary scheme Mark Twain proposed was alive half a year later but came to naught finally. The idea was for five or six authors to write a story jointly. The plan was kept secret, except that Roswell Smith, Richard Watson Gilder, and Robert Underwood Johnson of the Century Magazine *knew of it, and Gilder served as intermediary as the details were worked out. All the authors would start with the same group of characters, perhaps members of one family; then independently each would lead the characters through approximately the same experiences. But Mark wanted to make the book a burlesque of the old-fashioned novel; Cable was sure "the thing must be a square, honest hurdle-race, but not a mule-race." As he saw it, the best possibilities were in letting each author in his own way show how in a special location and under particular circumstances a set of characters ceased to be European and became American. He suggested a definite plot which would bring two unrelated children to America and then allow each author to take them through a love affair and some sort of tragedy. Later Gilder offered a still more specific plan: A newspaper advertisement would ask for information on children who had been orphaned during their voyage to America.[27] Each story would be one answer to the inquiry—"they came to such and such a place & the results were so and so," as Cable had written Gilder on July 9. Frances Hodgson Burnett, who had been asked to be one of the authors, was ill; but the scheme died chiefly because it was like others Mark Twain concocted which looked less feasible on closer inspection.*

On February 14 Cable could report further improvement in his health. The next day he and Mark Twain went to New York.

Everett House
New York, Feb 16, 1884.

. . . I have just dined with Buel[28] and Clemens at the Union League Club; but when I come into my room & find no wife sitting there, or walk the gay streets & she is not at my side, I moan with the pain of her absence. . . .

I am stronger today. Mark Twain & I took a carriage & went to see General Grant today—whom Mark knows well, but he has been ill & was asleep & Mark will go to see him Monday morning. It's about a scheme that Mark & I are starting. I'll tell you about it later—a big show

for the relief of the Ohio river overflow sufferers—Gen/l
Grant to preside & Mark Twain, Henry Ward Beecher
and I to furnish the entertainment at the Academy of
Music, New York. It may all fall through or it may work
—don't know, yet, which. . . .

*Cable had grown accustomed to the bantering and the
hilarity that accompanied Mark Twain wherever he went,
and he had discovered that he could hold his own in the
give-and-take customary with the man of solemn jest. Un-
intentionally he had provided Mark with a source of great
fun. One of those who came to see him while he was sick
was Dr. Francis Bacon of New Haven, who brought a
book entitled* Love Triumphant, or the Enemy Con-
quered.[29] *It was just the sort of absurd romance Mark
hated. He borrowed it to read at the next meeting of the
Saturday-Morning Club, and it was good for allusions in
the letters he and Cable exchanged afterward, though it
could not replace Bret Harte as a subject for his friends
to use in taunting him. The letter below tells of a joke on
Joseph Pennell, who had come to New Orleans early in
1882 to illustrate Cable's writings for the* Century Magazine *and before he left had grown fond of Cable and
certain of his literary future. Elizabeth Robins was Pennell's fiancée.*

Philadelphia, Feb 18, 1884.
. The interviewers are all gone. . . .
Tomorrow night my work begins again. I mustn't write
you at length tonight, but I must take time to say that the
big scheme falls through because Mr. Beecher had an
engagement that he could not possibly set aside. He was

very sorry, wanted to go into the scheme & thought we could raise $50,000 for the overflow sufferers. But it's all up & Mark's gone home.

I had not been here long when Pennell & Miss Robins called to see me. As quick as thought it came to me to jump into bed & pretend to be desperately sick. Pond rec'd them in the next room in a solemn whisper & let Pennell in. I fooled him finely. I jumped into bed clothes & all, covered up, & lay with the whites of my eyes turned up, my mouth open, gasping & moving my head from side to side & softly moaning. Poor Penn came in & stood by the bed. I slowly slipped my hand out from under the blankets. He took [it] & said softly—"Why, old fellow, I'm mighty sorry to see this"—Then I burst!

I don't believe it sounds funny to tell it, but it was *big* fun. . . .

Albany Depot, Ap'l 2, 1884.

. . . I reach Boston this afternoon. Tomorrow I read in Providence. I believe I read 3 or 4 times there & once in New Bedford.

. . . I wonder if it was mumps that first made me ill. For I have a letter from my dear, sweet little nurse who tended me with such faithful devotion, saying that she has had the mumps—took them soon after returning to the hospital. Two of Mark Twain's children had the petty plague of the same name, & Mark insists that I had it. My doctor said emphatically "no." . . .

One of Cable's jokes on Mark Twain was so successful that it was news for days in the papers over the country. Remembering the tirades against autograph seekers he had heard at the Clemens breakfast table, he sent a mimeographed letter to 150 of Mark's friends asking them to write for his autograph, timing their letters to reach him on April Fool's Day. Mark Twain gave the newspapers a report on the deluge of letters and telegrams and said he planned to exhibit them in Barnum's show. On April 8 Cable wrote home from New York: "I haven't said anything to you about the huge joke I played on him, for I doubted not you would hear of it through the papers." The next day: "Three interviews this morning. The newspaper 'boys' are wild over the Mark Twain thing." And on April 10: "The whole American literary guild is laughing over the Mark Twain joke." The episode bore open testimony not only that Cable and Mark Twain were intimate friends but also that Cable could keep pace with his friend in joke making.

Later in the spring when Cable planned to move his family north on a temporary basis, Roswell Smith proposed that Mark Twain locate a house for him in the vicinity of Hartford and that several of Cable's friends join together to pay the rent. Mark Twain wrote Pond on the matter. In his reference to Cable's reading at Hartford a year earlier and also in his opinion on the new proposal, Mark Twain reflected his habitual extravagance in seeing and in stating things.

May 15, [1884].

*My Dear Pond:

Roswell got up a Hartford-Cable-Lecture; & he put the Hartford end of it in my hands, & described how he was going to put the New York end of it through, himself. Do

* Copyright © by Mark Twain Company 1959.

you remember how he carried out his contract? *I* do—& don't you doubt it.

And now Roswell would put *another* project in my hands! Why, it almost makes me smile.

I have a great regard for him, & I do not hold any grudge against him for that thing; moreover, I would come forward & tackle any project of his that favorably impressed me. But this one does not. It is asking me to do a thing which I would not do for myself—nor for my father, if he were alive. It is a real estate agent's job— that is where it belongs; & a person of my unbusinesslike breeding could not fail to make a botch of it.

The other proposed feature is simply a crime against Cable's manliness. If a man should surreptitiously (or openly) pass around a hat in your behalf, would you ever forgive him for it? You know very well you wouldn't. Well, is Cable made of coarser clay? Let us hope not, & let us believe not. Your & Smith's project springs from a generous impulse, & does your hearts credit; but if it isn't a dishonoring one to the proposed victim, then my notions have somehow got a good deal distorted. Hang it, Pond, join me in a blush, & abolish that unspeakable proposition out of your mind. Let us be better friends to Cable than that. Individually, I could not think it right or fair or friendly to contribute money to Cable's support without first asking his permission; & if he granted it —— Oh, Good land, he *couldn't!*

In writing to Smith, I said nothing about the contribution-proposition, for I could not tell whether he was joking or not. I could by no means make out: & so was afraid to venture. But I pour myself out freely to you; it is the fair way & the right way—in fact the *only* square way.

Now here's *another* candidate for Hartford lecture-honors—George MacDonald. You see they *will* all pick out the worst town in America. Come, what do *you* say? If you wish to take him & run him around for the month of October, tell me so, & let me write him. And suppose you write him, too, if you think favorably of the thing.

    With great love to you both,

                        Mark.

The idea of paying the summer's rent for Cable was dropped, but a house was located for the Cables at Sims-bury, Connecticut. Cable wrote Pond of the affair:

                229 8th Street
           New Orleans May 19, '84.

Dear Major:

    ... Did you know that some of my friends North had a conspiracy for putting me into a summer home? Mark & his wife had gone & looked at the house. I knew nothing of it, but declined, on Mrs. Cable's account, to keep house. But when I knew that there had been a plot & that the plot had exploded & hurt no one & that Clemens & Mrs. Clemens had been pleased with the house I knew it must be a charming place for there are no such judges of housekeeping above ground, & I wrote to Mr. Smith to take it for me from July 1.

    Now I want you to keep me safe from conspiracies & the like. I know Mark wants my heart's best blood & I depend on you. Please keep them off. I am in earnest.

                      Yours truly

                      G. W. Cable

Mrs. Cable sends regards.

Before leaving with his family for Simsbury, Cable gave his first public reading in New Orleans. The reception given his program at Grunewald Hall was especially pleasing, for he knew that among the Creoles of his native city were some who resented his fictional portrayal of their history and character. The success of the New Orleans appearance was a heartening prediction of the returns Cable might expect from platform readings in the future.

229 8th Street
New Orleans, May 16, 1884.

Dear Major:

Last night was a royal triumph. The hall was full, full, to the doors and to the ceiling, and the audience was absolutely brilliant. Never have I enjoyed quite such a superb reception. Men stood against the walls clear around from the stage to the stage again. Extra chairs did not half accommodate the overplus. A committee of leading citizens formed the reception corps. This was notwithstanding the fact that there were two of the great social events of the season on hand, the Metairie Jockey Club free open air concert, & "Miss Stewart's ball." I enclose programme & clippings from T-Dem & Picayune. They called me out after the reading. I never suffered so from the heat before, and how the audience endured it I don't know; but the way they clapped and pounded would have done your big heart good. The advance sale was 427 seats at $1.25 each & would have been more but there were no more reserved seats to sell. There was considerably over $1000 in the house. It makes me laugh to think of the beaming patience with which that audience sat and roasted for two hours and a half.

Good-bye. I charged $150. The ladies must have *cleared* close to $700. I shall not repeat. The town will keep and ripen beautifully for next winter.

I want to write to Mr. Roswell Smith, must rush to a close. Photos rec'd. Everybody at home delighted with them. Yours is just what they had imagined you. Now, they want to see *you*.

Yours truly

G. W. Cable

Grunewald, the owner of the hall, says the audience was the largest ever gathered in the hall & it certainly was the finest.

THE HIGHWAY
ROBBERY BUSINESS

In the spring of 1884 Cable renewed his contract with Major Pond and could look toward the next season with pleasant assurance, for his success on the platform had far exceeded his expectations. Soon he heard from Pond that Mark Twain had a scheme that would tickle him. It was a scheme for a joint reading tour. Mark would take the risk, pay Cable $350 a week and expenses for twenty weeks. Cable hesitated, and Pond suggested as substitutes first James Whitcomb Riley, apparently, and then Thomas Nast. Mark Twain's directives to Pond in the letters below display his habitual impatience and abruptness in dealing with his business managers.

[Elmira, N. Y.] July 3 1884

*My Dear Pond—

I promised the other day, that I would not try to get anybody but Cable; & that if he declined to hitch team with me I would retire once more into my hole & keep away from the platform. So don't throw out any feelers toward Riley or make any propositions to him.—In the circumstances, you see, it wouldn't be worth while.

Yr truly
S L Clemens

Keep your hot weather—we haven't any on the hill, & don't need any.

[Elmira, N. Y.] July 8 1884

*Dear Pond—

O damnation, I would rather pay Cable $450 a week & his expenses than pay Nast $300.

I don't enjoy roosting around & waiting. If you are able to give me an ultimatum from Cable by the 15th of July (a week hence), all right; but I don't want it the 16th, because on that day I shall have made other arrangements.

Yr truly
S L Clemens

July 15/84

*Dear Pond—

All right. Webster will fix up the contract with you.

Give Geo. W. our love & the enclosed letter, & tell him we are all exceedingly glad the new house is satisfactory, & we propose to look in on him when we get back home.

If people begin to write me about these readings, I mean to forward the letters to you unanswered, & depend on you to answer them. Is that satisfactory?

Yr truly
S L Clemens

Before the end of the month contracts had been drawn on terms summarized in the following memorandum preserved among Pond's papers:

* Copyright © by Mark Twain Company 1959.

44

I have agreed with S. L. Clemens to furnish George W. Cable to him reading from his own works in joint entertainments for four months at $450 per week. And I have made this arrangement for Geo. W. Cable on the contract already made & now standing between us and am to be compensated according to the terms of that agreement. And I have further agreed that I will pay to George W. Cable one third of the amount of the compensation received from S. L. Clemens for my services to S. L. Clemens in the said arrangement; being ⅓ of 10% of the gross receipts.

The tour was eagerly reported in the newspapers from the start. In July the rumor was repeated in print that the venture was in the making. Pond's circular billed neither as the lead; they would divide the time on the stage, "so that the pathos of the one would alternate with the humor of the other, and the genius of both will be presented in a rapidly changing programme," to which the Lounger column in the Critic *remarked on August 9:[30] "I am at a loss to see how Major Pond is going to divide Mr. Cable so as to cut the humor out of him. To do this he will certainly have to give him very different selections to read from those that delighted Chickering Hall audiences last winter."*

The first appearance was in New Haven on November 5, the day following the national election. Early in the summer Cable had settled his family at Simsbury for a year, leaving undecided until later the question of whether to move permanently from the South. He had continued his voice training, first under Harold Henderson and later under his earlier teacher Franklin Sargent, and early in the fall he read in several halls alone. On September 26 he and Clemens met in New York to have a photograph made together for Pond's advertising.

Cable had already tried out on his audiences enough selections for two or three programs, but Mark Twain was a beginner at platform reading and had to make up his programs de novo. Since his beginning in California in 1866, Mark had become an experienced lecturer, but he would have to learn the art of public reading from Cable's advice and example. For one thing, he had to decide what type of matter and after that what specific pieces to read. A letter to Pond reflects part of his thinking.

Elmira, July 28/84

*My Dear Pond—

Yes, we want an advance-agent of course—I forGOT it.

Circular received. You want to say nothing about original sketches written specially for this series, for that is too decided a confession of weakness. It confesses that we know we can't draw just on our *names* alone, but have got to *add* something extraordinary to persuade the people to come.

I may possibly get up one or two original things for the series, but I shan't want the fact mentioned that they *are* new. I think it dangerous policy to let the public suppose we need any attraction but just our *names* alone.

With the corrections which I have marked in the proof I think the circular is good & all right.

Goodness knows *I* would gladly run 20 weeks, & I did my best to persuade the madam, but did not succeed. So that idea is killed. She almost said I might read again next

year if I didn't read too long this time, so I thought I
better not press the matter too far.

> Y truly
> S. L. Clemens

Mark Twain sent Cable proof-sheets of Huckleberry
Finn *asking for suggestions on what to read. One episode,
"King Sollermun," Cable replied on October 25, "is
enough by itself to immortalize its author," and he
thought Jim's account of his investments excellent for
the stage. He liked also the scene in which Huck concludes
that you "can't learn a nigger to argue," but he questioned
the use of the word "nigger" in the title, as Mark had intended, for it would appear in programs and in newspapers out of context and might offend needlessly. The
title was changed to "How come a Frenchman doan' talk
like a man?" All of these selections appeared in the programs Mark gave on the road.*

*The attention which Mark Twain gave to details of
the arrangements is indicated in a letter he wrote Pond
from Hartford on September 26:*

*Which reminds me. We *must* have programmes which
will not *rattle.* No paper allowed. Now set your invention
to work. A program can be rattled in our hall *one* evening, but that'll be the last time that that crime will be
perpetrated during our season.

Let me see. Programs might be printed on *cards,* one-
half the size of this envelope or this silhouette-card—too
small, you see, to be used as a fan.

If we send well-engraved small portraits ahead, with brief biographical sketches, country papers would insert them gratis in news columns, though city papers wouldn't.

A few days later he wrote:

Oct 84

*Dear Pond—

Letter rec'd last night—so I herewith send second day's program. I hoped Gilder & Cable were going to dig something out of Huck Finn for me to read; so I have waited. But only Cable has made a suggestion, & that happened by accident to be in a signature which the publisher has not sent me & continues to not send me, notwithstanding my implorings.

Pond, be sure & ask managers to print our programs on small coarse cards, can't you? things that people can't fan themselves with. . . .

Yo

Mark

P.S. This is a full 2-hour program, with no allowance for applause & a dozen other little eaters-up of valuable seconds & minutes; so, either Cable or I had better knock one 15-minute piece out of his program. If Cable objects to knocking it out of his, be sure you knock it out of mine. Knock out, "Why doan' a Frenchman talk like we does." The audience must go away hungry, not surfeited; & you know that after an audience has had about enough, every added minute acquires an ascending scale of weight, in pounds, just as the diamond does in carats; & to a well-tired crowd the next-to-the-last minute weighs upwards

* Copyright © by Mark Twain Company 1959.

of a ton. Harken to these wisdoms, dear sir & citizen, & act accordingly.

Yrs

Mark . . .

Mark Twain was convinced, as he indicated in writing to Pond late in October, that he would need to experiment with his selections and also with his presentation.

Hartford, Tuesday.

*Dear Pond—

It is now perhaps time that we three get together & have a *talk*. All has been done that can be done by correspondence; & has also been done as well as things can be done in that way. Now if you & Cable can run up here some day or night within the next 48 hours or so, without too much inconvenience, it might be a good enough thing to do. There is no rigorous necessity for it, of course, because such inconsequential errors as we might forestall by a talk, we can remedy as we go along through the preliminary small towns. Of course the appearing in half a dozen small towns first is for the *purpose* of weeding out errors: I understand that.

I got Cable's note yesterday, & do immensely approve of the change he suggests in the distribution of the stage-work. Let us stick to that plan—each to read a very short piece first; then Cable to bunch the rest of his time together; & afterwards I follow him & bunch all my remaining time together, & so close the performance. (Though I make *one* exception to this rule—see my program

49

marked "4th Day," herewith enclosed.) Wish to read "Tom as King" *first*.

Yes—"carriages at 10"—advertise that, always.

I sent you programs for 1st & 2d Days—but the one for 2d day I think I afterward corrected to what it now is (herewith enclosed).

I now send you programs for the *5 first appearances*—thus I appear in a *new program every night* for the first five nights. Careful note must be taken of the piece *which takes* BEST *every night* during the five—& then we will make up a *permanent one-night* program out of the pieces thus *elected*. See?

Yrs
Mark

Cable had first met Dr. Francis Bacon and his wife late in March, 1883, when he came to New Haven with introductions from President Gilman of Johns Hopkins University. Bacon had visited him later when he was sick in Mark Twain's house, and for many years afterward whenever Cable passed through New Haven he had a warm invitation to stop with the Bacons. During the joint reading tour, it was necessary to decline much of the entertainment that was proffered, in order to conserve strength. The day before the tour opened Cable had written his wife from New York: "the tax on my nervous strength is such that even I am fearful of the result unless I throw overboard every particle [of] work I can."

New Haven Conn Nov 6, 1884.
The work has begun. Mark & I read last night together. It was an emphatic success. Mrs. Clemens was present.

After the reading they came with me here to the Bacons
& the five of us sat down to tea. Oh! how I did want you!
Can't you meet me at Springfield tomorrow (Friday)
evening? . . .

Springfield, Mass. Nov 7, 1884.

I can't stop now to write. Have just read your letter. I
am very well & have got well started without fatigue.
Matters are being managed very systematically & every
day I feel better than the day before. Had a great success
in Orange last night.

Love & kisses to the precious little ones. I cannot say
yet when I can reach home. Enclosed find list of dates to
guide you in writing letters. . . .

En route bet Worcester & Providence
Nov 8, 1884.

I rested well last night and feel all right today. Must go
upon the platform twice before I lie down for the night.
Last night's performance in Springfield was against ter-
rible odds—brass music & fire-works in front of the hall,
vast crowds blocking the streets and cannon firing directly
in the rear of the house.

Still I did well & so did Mark, though not his very best.
Mrs. Clemens came up from Hartford with Mrs. Geo.
Warner; but this was the last chance she was to have of
hearing Mark. . . .

Providence, Nov/r 9th, 1884.

. . . Have passed a pleasant Sabbath. Yesterday's double
duty did not hurt me at all. I never did my work before
so brilliantly. You will be proud when I tell you that

Mark & I seem to divide the honors as nearly even as two men well could. Mark seems greatly pleased with my work, as I am with his. As I came off the platform yesterday afternoon followed by a tremendous clatter of applause & he met me in the door as he was going to take my vacated place he exclaimed, "superb! superb!" Even Pond, sitting back at the rear of the house, applauded—first time he has ever done it. One lady—when I read "Mary's Night Ride," quite lost herself and wrung her hands hysterically. But let's pass all that & talk about today.

This morning went out for a walk & to find a Sunday school—but these are held here in the afternoons. Fell in with young Karl Strakosch who is our "advance man" & had a pleasant walk in the crisp morning air. Came back & went to church—Episcopalian. Heard a good sermon on honest doubt. (Help thou mine unbelief.)

Music mechanically good but rendered without sentiment. After dinner (Mark being still abed) went to Sunday school—Baptist. Was instantly recognized & dragged into harness. Got away at 5 o'clock. I compelled the Sup/t not to give my name & so felt easier. One don't want to feel that he is advertising himself in Sunday School. Addressed the school incognito for ten minutes & was charmed, myself, to see how entertained & instructed they seemed to be. And it's a great comfort, in the midst of this "entertainment-giving" to get a chance to say an earnest word to seekers after truth. Goodbye, Mark is up, walking the floor in his night-shirt, smoking & talking. . . .

Cable's other Sundays on the road followed much the same routine as this. A member of the Presbyterian

Church and an elder since 1882 he was unwavering in following the rules of his church. It was his habit every Sunday to attend Sunday School and the two regular church services, though he went more often to some other church than the Presbyterian when he was away from home. When Pond told Mark Twain at the time the contract was being drawn that Cable would not travel on Sunday, he replied, "Well, I guess I shall meet him in heaven, finally. I had some fears on the subject."[31]

"Mary's Night Ride" was a selection from Dr. Sevier, Cable's novel published on the eve of his tour with Mark Twain. A tense episode in which Mary Richling rode with her child through the battle lines during the Civil War to reach her dying husband in New Orleans, this selection was a favorite with the audiences and was likely to be requested if it was not in the announced program. It seems to have been more popular, in fact, than any other number read by him or Mark Twain.

After a week on the road Mark Twain felt more assurance about his programs, as he showed in writing Pond. Earlier he had decreed that under no circumstances was Hartford or Elmira, New York, Olivia's home town, to be included in the itinerary, but he had other plans for two connected intimately with his early life, Hannibal and Keokuk.

Bos Nov 11/84

*Dear Pond—

Enclosed the programs for 2 New York Nights. The one for the *first* night is perhaps a trifle stronger than the other—& if it isn't, I learned last night how to *make* it so, (while on platform).

Now you can furnish these to the next five or six towns —first one & then the other, turn about, (every other night) so as to keep me familiar with *both* & always "up" in my part for *"2"*-night towns.

After a week, the same programs can be furnished to a lot of succeeding towns, if I find by that time that they satisfy me.

Here is a letter from my brother, in Keokuk, Iowa, where my mother lives. One of the dates he mentions as being open, is Jan *13*. Now how would it do to read in Hannibal, Mo. (where I spent my entire boyhood, in company with Huck Finn & Tom Sawyer) *Monday,* Jan 12,— then run up & read in Keokuk Tuesday night Jan 13? I'd like that, IMMENSELY. BOTH TOWNS.

Yrs Truly
Mark.

We will have no Place Congo music *in the programs*— Cable is going to slam that in as a gratuity, at the right time, on the platform. Good idea.

No mention of MR. Cable going to do any singing.

Mind you—in Hannibal you are not to sell the show; no, just write to John H. Garth (old schoolmate of mine,) & ask him to put you in communication with proprietor of Opera House or hall. We will run the show ourselves. I think this will be best, for the reason that I shall give all my share of the proceeds to some charity of the town— no money to be carried away except yours & Cable's.

Place Congo was a square in New Orleans where in earlier days the slaves gathered to sing and dance. From his first stage readings Cable had sung Creole songs but had as a rule introduced them only as encores.

The programs were arranged so that Cable always led off, each appeared four times, and Mark Twain closed the evening. Cable's last number was usually "Mary's Night Ride," and when he was called back to the stage he as a rule sang Creole songs. The following program, taken from the sheets handed out in Association Hall, Philadelphia, November 21, is the one they gave most often. On November 16 Mark had written of it to Pond:* "There will not be a Single Change made in it for a month to come—*it will* always *be our one-night & first-night program*."

1. From Dr. Sevier. Narcisse and John and Mary Richling. "Mistoo 'Ichlin', in fact, I can baw that fifty dolla' f'om you myself."

   Geo. W. Cable.

2. Advance Sheets from Huckleberry Finn.—"King Sollermun."

   Mark Twain.

3. From Dr. Sevier. Kate Riley, Richling and Ristofalo.

   Geo. W. Cable.

4. Tragic Tale of a Fishwife.

   Mark Twain.

5. From Dr. Sevier. Narcisse Puts on Mourning for "Lady Byron."

   Geo. W. Cable.

6. A Trying Situation.

   Mark Twain.

7. From Dr. Sevier. Mary's Night Ride.

Geo. W. Cable.

8. A Ghost Story.

Mark Twain.

After the first of the year the last number on this program was usually entitled "Selection" on the printed program. Cable's four numbers, all from Dr. Sevier, *had the merit of newness. In the character of Narcisse Cable presented the young Creole blade in his most delightful turning of phrases and ideas. The second of his readings displayed his skill—as both writer and reader—in handling the Irish dialect of Kate Riley and the Italianate speech of Ristofalo. Mark Twain's selection from* Huckleberry Finn *was even newer than the pieces from* Dr. Sevier, *for the book was not off the press until late in the tour. Mark Twain's second and third readings were from* A Tramp Abroad (1880). "A Ghost Story" *was one to give his audience a final thrill. It told how the coins had been stolen from the eyes of a corpse, and how the ghost cried out, "Who's got my money?" After that question had been repeated several times, with growing ominousness, Mark burst out, "Boo!"*[32]

In Philadelphia again five days later, they gave a second of their programs:

1. From Dr. Sevier. Narcisse's Views on Chirography. Raoul Innerarity Announces His Marriage.

Geo. W. Cable.

2. Desperate Encounter with an Interviewer.

Mark Twain.

3. From Dr. Sevier. A Sound of Drums.

Geo. W. Cable.

---

4. Certain Personal Episodes.

Mark Twain.

5. From The Grandissimes. Selection.

Geo. W. Cable.

6. Why I Lost the Editorship.

Mark Twain.

7. From Dr. Sevier. Mary's Night Ride.

Geo. W. Cable.

8. A Sure Cure.

Mark Twain.

As the season progressed, the third of their programs was altered more than either of the other two. From Detroit on February 12 Cable remarked that this program was "too uncertain in its effects; sometimes very good & sometimes poor." He kept "Mary's Night Ride"; he used Narcisse also, in a scene at the inundation or at the French Market; he included Raoul Innerarity exhibiting his picture or announcing his marriage. From The Grandissimes he introduced the most charming of his young Creole women, Aurore Nancanou, in the courtship scene with Honoré Grandissime; and at times he used "A Sound of Drums," a stirring war scene from Dr. Sevier. Mark Twain's most successful piece in this program was "Huck Finn and Tom Sawyer's Brilliant Achievement," recounting their fantastic maneuvering to free Jim late in Huckleberry Finn. "The Jumping Frog" story appeared regularly, and by the middle of February "The Blue Jay's Mistake" had been introduced from A Tramp Abroad. Cable related long afterward[33] how at his suggestion one night in Toronto Mark Twain had begun his program with the yarn about the blue jay. As he remembered the incident, Mark had been abusing him-

self, saying that he had made the audiences laugh at trivial matter which they would forget before the next day. Then Cable assured him that the following night he could draw no less laughter with selections of real literature. Whether Cable's memory was accurate in every detail after twenty-five years, there can be little doubt that he remembered the essentials of the incident. A further modification of the third of their programs in their last two weeks on the road suggests that both were concerned to put into it the best of their writings. The fact that the numbers were cut from eight to six suggests also an attempt to develop each piece more adequately as a literary selection. The printed program at Baltimore on February 27 was as follows:

1. Narcisse Puts on Mourning for Lady Byron.

    Geo. W. Cable.

2. Huck Finn and Tom Sawyer's Brilliant Achievement.

    Mark Twain.

3. Aurore and Honore, Courtship Scene.

    Geo. W. Cable.

4. The Blue Jay's Mistake.

    Mark Twain.

5. Mary's Night Ride.   .

    Geo. W. Cable.

6. The Jumping Frog.

    Mark Twain.

Boston, Nov 14, 1884.

We had a great time last night. Twenty-two hundred people applauding, laughing & encoring, in Music Hall. This morning Clemens & I go out to make a call or two.

Tonight we read in Brockton. Tomorrow afternoon & night in Chickering Hall. Our show is a great success.

It isn't easy to write as Mark Twain is singing "We shall walk through the Valley."

. . . Should you feel safe in doing so, & will telegraph me here (Parker House) you can meet me & spend Sunday with me in Worcester. I cannot get nearer than that to you except by nicking the edge of Sunday. Cars reach there from Boston at midnight & leave Monday morning at 6 1/2 o'clock. I shall take them en route for New York. . . .

Slack attendance at Brockton, Massachusetts, on November 14 and also at Boston the following afternoon prompted Mark Twain to rush instructions to Major Pond.

Boston, 15th.

*My dear Pond—

Louder advertising is absolutely necessary. We *must* have, in *every* town & city, one or two or half a dozen vast red posters with the single line,

MARK TWAIN——CABLE

Nov. 16—Op. House

—little poster at bottom for date & place, as above.

And we must have men to patrol the streets with billboards on their backs. We must resort to *any* methods— & if we then still have such houses as we had to-day & last night, it will mean that we can't draw & better quit.

Hurry up, old man!

Yrs truly
Mark.

The next day Mark Twain wrote Pond again: "Advertise with that big red line—that poster I spoke of—& with board-carriers." Cable's reports continue:

[On back of program for Association
Hall (Philadelphia), Nov. 21, 1884]

Mark is on the platform, there goes a roar of applause! We have a superb audience—both in numbers & quality —& we are beating ourselves. Mark says as he passes me on the retiring room steps "Old boy, you're doing nobly."

Somehow I struck a new streak yesterday evening at Newburgh. We had a little audience & no end of fun. They kept calling us back—There goes another round of applause. The laughter is almost continual & even my milder humor is interrupted with laughter & applause. There they go again! The hall is a large one with two large balconies reaching twice around from stage to stage & full to the ceiling. Men standing thick in the back of the house.

I thought you'd like to get just one letter from me from the lecture hall, so here it is. There they go again! . . . I closed because Mark was finishing, but they have called him back & he is reading the Investment of Fourteen Dollars, the same I told you of. . . .

Philadelphia, Nov. 22, 1884.

I can only write a line this morning. We are on the way to Brooklyn. Must go Monday morning to Washington. Be there Tuesday & in Phila. Wednesday. . . .

New York, Nov 23, 1884.

. . . Off in the morning early for Washington City. Shall

end the week in Baltimore. Shall probably begin the next week in Adams, Mass. if it can be reached by starting from Balt/o Monday morning 30 minutes after midnight. Maybe this would give you a chance to see me for a few hours in Adams. . . .

Washington, D.C., Nov. 24, 1884.

I am just in from the Reading. A crowded house that went off like gunpowder the moment it was touched; a *delicious* audience. The brightest, quickest, most responsive that we have yet stood before. As for me I certainly never before did such good work as I did tonight.

When I arrived in town the local manager told me he had between 12 & 15 requests for me to sing Zizi. The audience encored it; but I gave them "Mary's Night Ride" & then they encored that, & I sang Aurore.[34] How I do love to read the Night Ride; but it is a good half-day's work crowded into seven minutes. . . .

There must have been twenty persons in the retiring room. . . .

Washington, D. C., Nov 25/84.

I can only send a kiss. This is my 10th letter this morning. I have been cleaning up my neglected letter file. . . .

D. C. Nov 25/'84.

I am back in my room after our closing reading in Washington. What a good time we have had! . . .

Our reading was as crowded & as successful as last night. When I came off the platform after my second number whom should I find in the retiring room but the President of the United States, with Miss Frelinghuysen[35] & another lady whose name I missed. They went in between that number & Mark's 2/d & took seats amid applause. After the reading they came back the same way. The President showed himself very familiar with my works. He said "Yes, and the poor child! (Mary Richling) to find her husband dead after all!" We had a pleasant talk all round & then they took carriage & were off. . . .

Good night. Tomorrow we are off for Philadelphia. Next day to Morristown, N. J. where we dine with Thomas Nast. . . .

Phila. Nov 26, 1884.

If I don't write now I must steal bedtime hours & have done as much of that as I can afford. I have just read 1st number on 2d programme of today. A beautiful house very full. A pretty sight.

I wrote you last in Wash/n. I didn't tell you that I met Fred. Douglass. He came into the retiring room & was there when the President was there. They met as acquaintances. Think of it! A runaway slave!

Mark is on the stage reading (reciting) his "Desperate Encounter with an Interviewer," and the roars of laughter fall as regularly as a surf. I think it's a great thing to be able to hold my own with so wonderful a platform figure.

I have a letter today informing us that President-elect Cleveland will attend our Troy reading Dec 2.

Well, good night. We shall probably pass right through Simsbury—at least I shall, Monday morning. You must join me & go to Adams. I'll let you know what train. . . .

Baltimore, Nov 28, 1884.

I am well. Please consider this a telegram, not a letter. I can't find time to write today. Have written 19 business letters in the last 48 hours. . . .

Balt/o Nov 28, 1884.

I am again in the retiring room. Mark is making the house roar as only a Southern audience can. It is an immense house too, although the rain has poured all day long.

They have just encored me after Ristofalo's Courtship & from experience I safely judge neither Mark nor I will be without an encore to each number from this time to the end.

I am well & hardening to the fatigues of this life. So is Clemens. I expect to pass through Simsbury on Monday at 12/29, I believe. You can have all the children down at the station, can't you? And you'll go with me to Adams won't you? . . .

We had a jolly time with Nast & his family. He lives in simple elegance at Morristown & is not only jovial himself but has a family that are all like him; a wife, three daughters & two sons. Good night. I am back again in my hotel room. It was as I said. We could not respond to all the encores. Two readings tomorrow & then the sweet day of rest. Pres't Gilman came into the retiring room. How glad I was to see him. Mark & I dine with him Sunday. I shall go to church with him. Good night. G.W.C.

Thomas Nast's political cartoons were appearing regularly in Harper's Weekly. *Mark Twain and Cable stayed overnight in his home, and Mark made the occasion*

*memorable when, unable to sleep, he decided to stop all
the clocks or remove them from the house. The drawing
Nast made afterward showed Mark carrying the clocks
and Cable holding a candle, both in nightshirts.*[36]

En route betw'n Albany & Ithaca
Dec 3, 1884.

We got to Albany without delay. . . . At 3/30 we all—a
party of seven or 8 went in carriages to the capital &
called on President elect Cleveland. What a slander his
pictures are of him. He has one of the strongest and most
remarkable faces I have ever seen. He looks like a born
ruler and a great soldier. His face is one that one is satisfied should be the face of the nation's chief magistrate.
Best of all its strength, though it does not lack intel-
lectuality, is mainly moral. I studied it well while we
talked, and I came away from it with the strong conviction that the vile tales that have been told of him are
merely vile tales. His manner and speech are those of a
man to whom great things are easy. Now we shall see, in
the four years to come, whether physiognomy is worth
anything.

We had 1400 hearers at Troy. Mark was half sick with
a cold—hoarse and weak-voiced, and compared with
Balt/o & Wash/n the evening's success was feeble; but
the audience thought it was great. Mary's Night Ride had
to go without an encore at last. But it wasn't my fault
and it was the hit of the evening. The Ghost Story
(Mark's) fell almost flat by reason of *persons* (2 or 3)
rising in the audience just at the critical moment. It was
outrageous & I don't wonder M. T. came off the platform
angry. This whole Albany-Troy day & night has been one

long succession [of] the most flattering public and private attentions. I cannot tell you all about them, for want of time. Suffice to say my mind is full, this morning, of the flitting images and echoing voices of pretty girls, young men's wives and men who had "read everything we had ever written" &c &c &c. We were given a nice little supper & got to bed at the neat hour of two o'clock, with Mark at peace under the influence of our solemn pledge to each other henceforth to stop our reading and poke unmerciful fun at any one who dares to rise in the audience while we are speaking. It is our only defense against this double imposition on the audience and us. . . .

Syracuse, N.Y. Dec 4, 1884.

At Ithaca we stopped with Mr. Henry M. Sage, once a partner of Clemens' father-in-law, Mr. Langdon. . . .

At the opera house we had a good time. Found a quiet, undemonstrative audience and presently had them clean out of themselves. The encores were plentiful. Tonight, here in Syracuse the house, they say, is not going to hold the people. We shall see. . . .

Utica, Dec 5, 1884.

Had our usual good time in Syracuse, though the house was not entirely, but only almost, full. We find the audiences out here cold, but we soon warm them up. . . .

Rochester, N.Y., Dec/r 7th, 1884.

We could not be together today—the fifteenth of our wedding days. . . .

Now let me tell you of my journeyings. In Utica . . . the audience was large & the evening a bright and successful one, fully up to our high mark.

Rose at 4/30 A.M. and took cars for here. Arrived at 10 A.M. . . . Went at 2 P.M. to matinée, in a pouring rain. Audience small for the first time since our first ½ week; but appreciative to a degree. At night, rain still pouring down, had a large house and great fun. I think that, for all I may have said in previous letters, I never before did so well. Mark did ever so well, too. . . .

. . . What a happy sabbath I have spent. Mark Twain I have not seen since this morning, the hotel people having put us on different floors instead of in adjoining rooms as usual. I am told the papers say he was to have enjoyed the hospitality of a club, The Elks, this evening. It may be so. But I feel sure his Sunday has not been happier than mine. Oh! how I wish he were a man of prayer & worship. But he has more nobleness of nature & is more to be admired than I knew before now. . . .

No other of Cable's numbers was more popular than the Creole songs, except possibly "Mary's Night Ride." Not infrequently requests for songs were received ahead of a program, and regularly he sang one or two or even three of the songs when he was encored. His usual procedure was to give first a free English translation before singing in the Creole patois. A description of the singing which H. C. Bunner wrote his friend Walter Learned suggests the enthusiasm the songs won in Cable's listeners:

But the singing—that caught everybody. It was absolutely artless. He took the key as a kind Providence gave it to him. If it didn't happen to be the right one, he cheerfully announced the fact, and made a new guess for the next verse. But the *go*, and the lilt, and the solid, keen enjoyment he took in it! And the strong, pulsing wild melodies! Nigger from the ground up, and full of life. The huge house woke up as if you had turned a dynamo on it.[37]

Cable grew more and more uncomfortable about the songs. Major Pond, interested mainly in his drawing power at the door, warmly defended the singing; Richard Watson Gilder thought his reputation as an author would suffer. The songs were not curtailed during the joint tour, but soon afterward Cable dropped them from his repertoire and only upon special occasions and special request did he sing afterward on the platform.

Toronto, Dec 8, 1884.

Such a time as we are having! Such roars of British applause. I never heard anything like it out of N. Orleans. Mark is reading. I have just read Kate Riley & Ristofalo, interrupted by roars of laughter and applause.

We are in a big glass Horticultural Hall with people so far away at the bottom of the audience that their features can hardly be discerned. . . .

When I go back upon the platform again (in a moment) I have to sing my 2 or 3 Creole songs. I always shrink from this, the only thing I do shrink from; though it's always encored.

There! Mark is encored. But he'll be off in a minute.

Well, I'm off—2 songs & an encore. Mark is on. So we go. . . .

Buffalo, N. Y. Dec 10, 1884.

Back under our own flag. Enjoyed Toronto greatly. The citizens paid us all the attention we could receive and offered much more. Were driven out yesterday morning to see the city. . . .

We had much such a reception on last night as the night before. The audience was larger. I think I did hardly so well, though I do not know that the audience found it out. They did not show it, at least.

Off and away this morning. Clemens stays on the Canada side until this evening for copyright reasons. Huck Finn is being published in London today & he must be on British soil. . . .

. . . I have a great pleasure in store for tomorrow. I am not only to share with Mark T. the reception of the Thursday Club after the reading, but I am to attend a little parlor play at 3 P.M. at which some young ladies are to act a scene selected from *The Grandissimes*.

From here we go Thursday night to Ann Arbor, where, I hear, a great enthusiasm awaits us. . . .

Buffalo, N. Y. Dec 11, 1884.

I notice my letters have lately fallen into the shape of a diary, but I dare say you will like them so. . . .

Last night we had great fun. For a week past we have been introducing one another on the platform in our two opening numbers, simply saying, "Ladies and gent/n allow me to introduce to you, —————." But last evening to my astonishment Mark launched out into a burlesque introduction that filled the house with laughter; but I was [in] luck nevertheless, for just at the end of his little speech he really without intention betrayed a little opening in his harness and in went my dagger and the laugh was turned upon him in a torrent. The whole evening was a great success from a literary standpoint; but the house was not full. Yet there were many hundred present and they had an uproarious time. "Mary's Night Ride" went off with its usual, or even more than its usual, effect. As I said "And they made it!" a big man in the front row of seats jumped in his chair and holloed out "good!" so loudly that he was heard all over the house. So much for my morning letter; I'll resume later in the day. I wish you could see our beautiful suite of rooms.

Mark & I went & lunched with David Gray. . . .

Mark came back to the hotel. Mrs. Gray & I went to the gathering where I was to see Aurore & Clotilde[38] in their various scenes. Well, it was, of course, a school-girl affair, but there was much about it that was bright & clever. The girls were well "made up" for their parts & Aurore had a pretty continuous sparkle of eyes, gesture & voice. The dialect was so so—too slow, not crisp enough. . . .

Ann Arbor, Mich., Dec 12, 1884.

I cannot write a letter; my head aches & I am just putting myself tenderly to bed to try & sleep off the ailment.

Came from Buffalo this morning, leaving there at 12/30 last night, and am feeling as one is apt to feel after a night in a sleeping-car.

We accepted too much pleasant attention in Buffalo & so have to turn our backs on everything here, even the invitation of the President of the University—Pres/t Angell[39]—to meet Mrs. Ex-president Hayes at dinner.

They say our audience tonight will number 2500 persons. . . .

Leaving Ann Arbor, Mich., Dec 13, [1884].

Once more on the road. . . .

My experience of Ann Arbor has been as different from my last spring's as can be.[40] But what a crop I have harvested from that last spring's seed. The instant I spoke to the audience I saw that they were bent on obliterating the past; and they did it nobly. Rarely have we read to an audience of such combined discrimination & enthusiasm. Never have I met with equally *prized* applause—at least not out of Boston & N. York. In the Kate Riley courtship scene I was at one point interrupted by applause so long that for the first time in my experience I had to abandon my impersonation of the character and stand & wait until they would let me resume. Mary's Night Ride received a double encore. We were kept 30 minutes longer on the platform than we had expected to be. It is astonishing how much like the steady tumble of the surf the laughter was when Mark was reading.

We went, after all, when the entertainment was over, to Prof/r & Mrs. Rogers' reception given to Mrs. Hayes. The ex-mistress of the White House is a fine lookng woman. . . .

It was quite a brilliant company; University professors & their picked friends; some very bright & pretty girls among mothers & aunts, fathers & bachelors. We got away very early & went to the tavern & to supper. A deputation of students waited to see us in the parlor. Rec/d them standing and after some pleasant exchanges parted from them & went to bed, where there was rest from the incessant apologies offered me for last spring's miscarriage. They don't know that on that evening, for which they express so much mortification, I was paid $175.

But they are right; I told Pond then, I wanted no more like it at that price. . . .

I pause here. I see I've formed the habit of writing you a mere diary; but it is about all one can do on the railroad cars. . . .

Grand Rapids, Dec 14, 1884.

Here I am spending the Sabbath. Our rooms are very comfortable and the snow is falling outside, now lightly and now very heavily. Went to church this morning to a large Baptist church the hour being late and that church being just at hand. Something funny happened: I went down into the Sunday-school after church, unrecognized. Sat near the door in an adult class (male). A lady teacher said good-morning. Still unknown. The preacher came round. Asked me if I was a stranger. Yes. Where did I live? O, a great way off; just in town for a day; tho't I'd drop in &c. But he would have my name & town. I gave it—joy! still unrecognized! Presently he came back. "Did you say you were from New Orleans?" "Yes." "Do you, or did you ever, know a gentleman there named Sevier?— Dr. Sevier?" "No, sir." He looked me in the eye. I did as much to him. Then he said, "Is Dr. Sevier dead?" "Yes, sir." I threw up the sponge. He got me upon the platform. I said a word or two to the school on the lesson, and went back to the class. The lady teacher was the pastor's wife. She insisted on my teaching the class, but I insisted hardest, on her teaching it. By and by I was taken off to address the infant class. The dear little tots! The pastor wanted me to address the congregation tonight, which he said would be a very large one of young people; but I told him I thought as talking was my daily toil I ought to rest from it on Sunday evening.

71

We had, last evening one of those audiences that had to be lifted out of its apathy and estrangement; but we did it and secured the usual results. . . .

The day draws to its close. Clemens & Pond have left me. They will soon be on their way to Toledo by rail. I follow them early tomorrow morning. We read tomorrow in Toledo & Tuesday in Detroit; Wednesday in Cleveland and Thursday in Elmira. On Friday I reach N. York & read before the Y.M.C.A. and meet my blessed wife.

This hasn't been one of my best Sundays. I do not feel that spiritual refreshment I want. But the next one, God willing, will be spent with you in our quiet valley home among our five darlings and our gentle, quiet friends. . . .

Toledo, O, Dec 15, 1884.

Here's the platform again, with a thin audience in front of it which we have got to wake out of the depths of apathy. I haven't read so poorly since Springfield as I seem to be reading tonight. I have done half my work on the programme, and Mark is out doing the last number of his first half.

I began to write as soon as I came in, but as I write I see that my effect has already been felt, for they are responding to Mark from the very start. Our experience with such houses is that I lift them a little with my first number, then he lifts them from that stage a little higher, then with my 2/d number I lift them to a third elevation & with his 2/d no. (being the 4th) he gets them into a good strong glow. I am happy to see it is working just so now, after all. If he can get an encore from them on this we shall have them to the end without trouble.

There! Mark gets the call back twice over. Now we're all right. It will be encores right through to the end.

It turns out as I said; each one called back at the end of each number. First M.T. & then I & now Mark again. I have only Mary's Night Ride left to do; & it will be the 40th time I shall have done it.

There, I'm through, with the usual success. . . .

Toledo, O. Dec 16, 1884.

I enclose one of those time-killers that I find relief in writing in the retiring room. I hope you don't tell anybody what sort of letters I write you. I write about myself and this circus of ours because I know every word concerning it and me is interesting to you. I dare you to say it isn't!

This place is the place of residence and of daily labor of the famous Petroleum V. Nasby (Mr. Locke).[41] He is a big man with disheveled hair, knotted forehead, heavy middle and dowdy dress. An easy talker, a coarse man of the harder world, successful and unsatisfied.

"I'll tell you, Clemens," he said, "I've settled down upon the belief that there is but one thing in this world better than a dollar, and that's a dollar-and-a-half." But he is, maybe, less sordid than he pretends. How the fine lines—so often hid from view in Mark's face—did shine out as I compared the two men.

Nasby (or Mr. Locke) took us to his club house to a pleasant supper of birds &c. He quite astonished us with the account of his successes with the Toledo *Blade*. His weekly "Blade" had in September last a circulation of 200,000. He says he has sold it out four times and had to take it back within two years every time. Once he sold it with a circulation of 80,000 & in 13 months took it back with a circulation run down to 27,000.

He is 2 years older than Mark, but shows not a grey hair. He says, "I shall live till the circulation of the Toledo Blade is a million." I don't know what arrangement he has made with Providence, but he spoke very confidently.

He told us something else: Beside his plate stood a large glass of some outlandish drink placed there in response to his order "Mix me my regular swash." Presently he said, "Clemens, I guess you—who've seen me drink in other days, when for twenty years I never went to bed one single night truly and duly sober,—you hardly expected to see me drinking only lemonade mixed with ginger ale, eh?" (You know ginger ale is a perfectly un-alcoholic effervescent drink.) Mark expressed his astonishment.

"Yes," said Nasby, "18 months ago I quit all in one day. I said, A man can't be a business man & a drunkard too, so I stopped. There was only one way; that was to stop at once & totally & forever, & I did it. In forty-eight hours I was able to eat a square meal & in a week I could wake at 3 in the morning and not have the horrors." I asked what he meant by the horrors, for I knew he did not mean "delirium tremens." He said, "I mean I did not want to commit suicide; that's what a drunkard wants to do before day in the morning." He said again, "Yes, but it was fearful work, quitting. About 3 or 4 o'clock every afternoon any drunkard who sits at a desk feels that he is going straight to destruction, financial, social, moral, all kinds. And he knows that two drinks will make him feel rich. He need only go across the street & take 1 drink & he will feel that matters are not bad after all. A second & he don't care what they are; a third and he owns all

Summit street for a mile, both sides! He went to take two; 'only *two?*' he says, and as sure as death he takes ten!

"I do not believe," he said—& you know that he & I are alike in this—"I do not believe in the appetite for drink. The truth is the drinking man has an unhappy *knowledge* that a craving which he feels can be cured for the moment with whiskey. But water or coffee or an orange or a lemon would cure it, too; *will* cure it! *does* cure it!" This is not all the truth but it is one side of it.

We had some laughs over the lecture business. He avers that he has actually delivered one old lecture, with the MS before him, 480 times! Said he, "I've given that lecture when I was so drunk that the audience was *invisible;* and I knew it was going right only by the laughter and applause coming up out of that rayless gulf at the proper intervals."

O dear! He went with us to our hotel & stayed until his cigar was only half an inch long. Then he said good-night. I'm glad he's gone. He's a bad dream. He laughed at us for confessing fatigue. Said he knew nothing about any loss of power on the platform from that cause.

We are on the cars, now, bound for Detroit. I shall meet friends there. I think we'll have a pleasant time. . . .

On December 19, during the ten-day Christmas vacation from the tour, Cable appeared alone at the Y.M.C.A. in New York. He told his hearers on that occasion that he missed having Mark Twain introduce him. "First he would introduce me," he said, "so that the audience would know which of us was which; and then I would introduce him—so that they would know which of us was the other."[42]

Dayton, O. Dec 30, 1884.

I am in from a very tiresome & unsatisfactory reading, with a head aching with fatigue. Ten hours railway travel is not a good preparation for the platform. . . .

Had a good time yesterday in Pittsburgh. Tell you about it some other time. . . .

Dayton, O. Dec 31, 1884.

So we end another year. It has been full of bounty to us. How much happiness—how little trouble have fallen to us. It is right and best that the future should be kept from our knowledge so that we may walk by faith & not by sight.

It is not easy to do this when all is prosperous. It is not easy to remember, humbly & practically, that it is not we who are providing, but a bountiful God. But we shall have opportunity enough the coming year.

In the first place all that I shall make beyond our living this winter will go to the payment of debts. I even hope to get so far on as to make a big hole in the mortgage on our house. Then, I must go back to my desk. There my earnings are not so great and we shall hardly be able to forge ahead. The chances seem to be that I shall be able simply to avoid falling behind. But you know we have agreed that I should (we should) never lay our plans in the mere light of pecuniary profits or selfish profits of any kind. We are just as completely dedicated to God's service as though we were Chinese missionaries. Am I not right? And so I shall do this year whatever seems to me—I hope I may say we shall do whatever seems to us—to be the best thing we can do for the greatest good of our fellow-creatures. And so we can't possibly know where we'll be or what we'll do or how much of this world's goods we shall have at another year's end; but must leave all this to Him whose servants & children we are.

I think I have done the best thing I could for everybody in taking this reading tour and so enlarging my circle of readers and giving me a fame which I hope to make profitable as a teacher of truth and religion. But I think I shall not go on the platform after this year, after this tour is finished. I don't think I shall be wanted by the public with sufficient desire to justify a tour. So we shall not, pecuniarily, swim in grease. We have got to—& I'm well satisfied that it should be so—we have got to walk in the dark. Our gracious Heavenly Father will make it light round about us.

Our children's schooling occupies my thoughts much. I long to give them the best. Let us save every penny we can for this end. I mean of course what we can save from our own comforts and indulgences.

I told you in last night's letter that we had a good time in Pittsburgh; & so we did. Not the best sort, however. We pleased our audience thoroughly & it was a large & cultivated audience. The newspapers, however, must have taken some grudge against us; for they made offensive reports of the affair. . . .

As it turned out, Cable did not give up the platform at the end of the tour. For several years his readings yielded his chief income, and after fifteen years he was still on the reading circuit, filling what engagements could be made profitable.

Paris, Ky, Jan 1, 1885.

I cannot let the 1st day of the year pass & write no

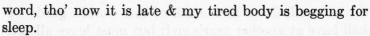

word, tho' now it is late & my tired body is begging for sleep.

We have just finished a delightful evening on the platform before a hearty, quick-witted audience that laughed to tears and groans at Mark's fun & took my more delicate points before I could fairly reach them.

I have a little bunch of flowers given me by a young lady of the Clay family. Many persons crowded round us after the entertainment. All this was particularly pleasing to me inasmuch as this is a Southern town & the two feelings which I always have to encounter in Southern towns were present & evident here. A ball was given in opposition.

We had a gay time last night, too, in Hamilton, Ohio. Some little boys paid us the highest compliment we have ever rec'd. They said, going home from the readings, they would rather go to hear us any time than go to any circus & one, not content with this, said he'd rather hear us than see "Buffalo Bill." . . .[43]

When Cable was ready to leave Cincinnati, after two evening readings and one matinée, on January 2 and 3, he wrote his wife, "We have had a great time here." Rested from the road by the Christmas holidays, he and Mark and Pond apparently had begun again with high spirits. They were registered at the St. Nicholas Hotel as "J. B. Pond and two servants." After the evening's reading on January 3 an interviewer for the Cincinnati Enquirer sat down with the three of them and also Ozias Pond, the Major's brother, who was ready to take over as traveling manager. They were in the dining room at the St. Nicholas, where Mark had a bottle of ale and Cable a dish of ice cream. Mark was asked about his days as a newspaper reporter; then about Bret Harte. His statement that Harte could not write dialect was banteringly disputed by Cable:

"There you go again on an argument," returned Mark Twain. "But I tell you when Harte tried to write frontier dialect it was idiocy. . . . Why, he could have taken it to any miner and had it remedied; but he did not."

Mr. Cable responded by grasping an empty ale bottle and threatening to break it over his companion's head.

Mark refused to say which he thought his best work, but Pond put in, "I think a sirloin steak is his best work." " 'No puns,' cried Clemens, as he grabbed his bottle and made a gesture toward his manager." When Cable was asked, after Mark had gone to his room, how he liked his partner, he answered: "We fight all the time. I think that in four three minute rounds with soft gloves I could knock him out; he's not much on science." Then after Cable had left the table, Major Pond had his say: "If you want to have fun, you ought to travel with us for a day. You would die. Now, I am really funny, very funny, but that pair have made up not to laugh at anything I do or say, especially if I perpetrate a pun. They think it great fun. That's their idea of enjoyment."

From Cincinnati on January 4 Cable wrote, "I have some noble letters from persons who have read my Freedman paper." The January Century Magazine *contained an essay of his entitled "The Freedman's Case in Equity," an earnest argument for extending greater civil rights to Negroes, which had stirred heated opinions immediately*

---

upon the appearance of the issue late in December and soon was to be discussed from one end of the country to the other.

The essay had been written for delivery before the American Social Science Association meeting at Saratoga the preceding September 11, but its growth in Cable's mind extended back much earlier. The son of slaveholders in New Orleans, he had raised no questions about slavery or the Southern attitude toward race until the years following the Civil War. Convinced by his own inquiry that the Biblical defense of slavery was weak if not indeed dishonest, and by his study of the Declaration of Independence and the Constitution that slavery was incompatible with the ground principles of the American government, he believed that the Negro race had suffered such wrong at the hands of the white race in America that reparation should be made however possible. At the very least the Negroes should be allowed full public rights. But such a view was so much out of line with the commonly expressed views in the South that Cable only slowly began debating the matter openly. In university commencement addresses in Mississippi and Louisiana and Alabama, in 1882 and 1883 and 1884, he had raised the question with progressively more directness. Then in accepting the invitation to address the Social Science Association on the subject, he determined to face the issue squarely and honestly, even at the risk, as he clearly recognized it, of alienating much of the sentiment in the South. In several of the following letters in this volume he tells his wife of the response his essay drew from the reporters who called on him, the editorial writers of Southern newspapers, and those who came to discuss the subject in the cities and towns he visited with Mark Twain.

En route—Cincinnati—Louisville,
Jan 5 [1885].

We returned to Cincinnati on the evening of the 2d. . . .

We had hardly time to eat & dress for the platform. The hall is a new one, called Odeon. I stepped upon the stage at 8/05, the audience seeming to be about all in; but I had hardly begun offering a few words of preliminary explanation when the incoming of people grew so troublesome from their number that I stopped and said that as there were almost as many people standing as there were sitting, I would sit down a moment and let the aisles empty into the chairs. There was instant applause. I sat down & fully 200 people came in and found their seats. It seems the severity of the cold in some way caused the street cars to be in some way impotent.

When I rose again and said this was the first time I had ever attempted to read to a procession, there was great laughter & applause & my first number went off with the happiest effect.

A small matter to tell and only worth while because of the next afternoon's experience. When I got out on the platform the audience was all in and a most brilliant one it was. But again I had not finished my opening number when a piano somewhere in the building, behind & above the stage began to resound in most spirited fashion. I ceased, and stood listening, the audience sitting ready to burst into laughter if I should but give the word. I said, "I fear the audience cannot listen with intent appreciation to the reading and the piano at the same time, and so if you please we'll all sit down and listen to the music." Of course this simple gag brought long continued laughter, which ceased only when the unseen instrument languished for a moment, gave a little spasm and stopped.

It is a great mistake to suppose that these little accidents embarrass a ready-witted speaker; they are windfalls, & can almost always be turned to good account, putting the audience into familiar sympathy with him. That is, when they are not serious matters. Four times, now, it has happened that a lady had to be carried out, ill, & every time it has been during my reading of Mary's Ride; not attributable to it, but that being near the end of our two hours, the room warm & the air bad. It happened this time.

The other night, in Hamilton, O., a man with creaking shoes stalked out of the hall in the midst of one of Mark's numbers. You know I told you we had decided to give any such person a shot across his bows. So Mark calls out in the most benevolent & persuasive tone, "Take your shoes off, please; take your shoes off"—to the great delight of the applauding audience.

Saturday morning as I sat at breakfast quite late—10 o'clock—Pitts Burt came in and we went off at once to Mrs. Nicholls's famous pottery—Rookwood Pottery. . . .

Interrupted by arrival in Louisville. Have just lunched and must throw myself upon the bed & snatch a nap before the L'ville Press Club's reception to us at 4 o'clock. . . .

Got off early to go to church. . . .

Wandering along, I stumbled upon an African-Methodist-Temperance church. Can't tell you about that now; hope to tonight. . . .

Henry Watterson, owner and editor of the Louisville Courier-Journal, *was related to Mark Twain through the Lamptons, his mother's family.*

Galt House, Louisville, Ky.
Jan'y 6, 1885.

My hours are so full of experiences that I can scarcely find a moment in which to write you a line. We had a very rainy, muddy night last night, but a very large audience and a tremendous time. Uproarious applause. Every piece encored except the opening piece. Press Club gave us an afternoon reception and Henry Watterson carried us off after [the] readings to the Pendennis Club to a quiet supper by ourselves—we three only.

I had long been curious to see Watterson. He didn't please me. Talks shamelessly about getting drunk &c &c. Strange that such moral distortion can go with a certain large integrity & public honor but so it is at times. His face repeats his character; one eye sightless, the other painfully nearsighted and the flesh, from top of forehead to the much razored chin, hard, full of blood, and firm with headstrong purpose.

In the Press Club, fell into a discussion of the negro question. It makes one's teeth ache to get once more among a typical group of Southern men who steal glances at each other but not a man Jack of them will venture an opinion. Freedom of speech has yet to come to us of the South. Yet how far we have progressed beyond our old ante-bellum position; for I spoke with perfect freedom and gave no offense & two or three men even went so far as to say "We admit (&c) but how are you going"—&c? I'll come to better utterances in a few minutes.

Jan'y 7, '85.

Went from there to the Pendennis Club house just to register. . . .

At Watterson's little supper after the reading a man joined us. . . . Clemens & Watterson & I walked home. It was 1 A.M. At the doors of the *Courier-Journal* office Watterson said goodbye. "Now," said he, *"my* work *begins."* I woke & rose at 10.

At eleven was called for by Prof. Allmond & young Halleck, of the L'ville High School, & Mr. Cochrane, Pres/t of the School Board, to go & see the High Schools. I've never had quite such a time. Saw & addressed the boys first—some 300 bright fellows glad of any chance to laugh and clap their hands. I spoke for conscientious freedom of thought as a right & duty. Then went to see the girls—400 damozels. They sang "America," with great sweetness & charm. I got a bright laugh or two & hand-clappings from them & then gave them an earnest word on their responsibility as the custodians & arbiters of sentiment & exhorted them to strive for correctness in their methods of thought. But they must needs have me sing; & when I had sung they kept up such a persistent clapping that I had to sing again. Then a march was struck, on the piano, & they filed out in an extremely pretty involved movement among the pews & aisles of their chapel.

I was then taken into a room—where the class in literature recites & shown my picture hanging on the wall with my autograph letter under it, acknowledging their letter of thanks of last season.

Into the carriage again & off to the Colored High School, male and female in one. Here I confronted some 200 &

more scholars, all shades. They, too, sang "America" very prettily & correctly. I addressed them & was gratefully surprised to be told by the gentlemen who accompanied me that their own hearts echoed my words—for I tell you I didn't mince matters. The visit was a surprise to the school, yet a mulatto boy rose when I had finished & in a phrase or two that were simply perfect & which called forth the admiration of the committee, moved a rising vote of thanks. Then they sang a lovely psalm, "Praise the Lord for He is kind"—I could have cried. When they had marched out so did we, & at 2 P.M. got back to the hotel with barely time to eat before the hour for receiving a delegation of colored men coming to thank me for my "Freedman's Case in Equity."

They came at 3—yellow, black, brown, yellow, brown & black, seven or eight in number. After a grand shake-hands they all sat down & one—the blackest—rose & made a formal impromptu address of thanks that made [it] hard for me to hold down my feelings. I replied; there was some conversation & they rose to go. You would have not got off with dry eyes had you been there. One said, "Good-bye, my hero of heroes." I thought of the great dead—Lloyd Garrison, Wendell Phillips & the rest and felt ashamed to let them give such praise to me.

Clemens & I were invited to dine with Watterson at home, but I was worn out & had to let Clemens go alone & apologize for me. . . .

. . . Rec'd a newspaper correspondent for a few minutes, & then undressed, went to bed and slept sweetly for 2 hours. Rose, dressed, ate & with Clemens went off to the hall. It was crowded. Pond turned people away. This is the more remarkable as the whole season, so far, has been dreadful for the amusement business. There was more "money" in our house Monday night than in all the theatres combined, more still last night. The audience applauded as Clemens & I passed through into the greenroom. The gallery cheered on Monday night when I read "Mary's Night Ride," & last night they encored *every* appearance of each of us on the platform, even my first; and even though we declined repeatedly to respond.

After the reading we went to a reception and supper at the Pendennis Club, where I had such a delightful farewell reception last spring. . . .

. . . We had a noble time, and at nearly 1 o'clock, when the ladies & girls were actually standing with their hands in their muffs I had to pluck Clemens by the sleeve & point out the fact, before I could make him understand that I and everybody were waiting for him to say good bye. He laughed long when I said this morning, "Wouldn't there have been a scatteration if our wives could have dropped in on us? . . ."

I have written the most of this letter on the cars. We had to rise before six. Are now nearing Indianapolis. . . .

The Southern / St. Louis, Jan'y 9, 1885.

I get little chance to scratch a line. We have just reached the end, however, of our hardest journeyings and shall have some chance here to breathe.

. . . Interrupted by two interviewers. . . .

The reporters had come to ask him about the Freedman problem. On the train for Quincy, Illinois, on the twelfth, he wrote at length by way of advice about his children and added near the end, "I shall not go over the account

*of our reading in St. Louis. It would be the same old,
pleasant story." On other sheets, however, he had left a
record of one episode of the stay in St. Louis. At the
Southern Hotel James Lampton had come to call on
Mark Twain. While this aged but still recognizable original
of Colonel Sellers, in* The Gilded Age, *talked with Mark,
Cable listened through the door to his adjoining room,
purposely left ajar, and wrote down what he heard. Then
he was called into the room to meet Lampton and afterward he continued the record of Lampton's part of the
conversation. It was this visit which prompted Mark to
say long afterward that Lampton had not changed a jot
and that Colonel Sellers was an exact copy of him.*[44]
*Cable's partial transcription of Lampton's speech is of
special interest because it is apparently the only preserved
report of James Lampton aside from Mark Twain's own
statements. The following words of Lampton's are enough,
surely, to equate him with Colonel Sellers:*

Well, Mr. Cable I want you to come down with Cousin
Sa-a-am & see my daughters. They're school-ma'ams, you
know, self-sustaining institutions—women air, you know,
ah, ha, ha, ha! And if you'll come down to our very
plain little place—you're a Southern man & used to
rusticity—I'll take you down to the edge of my pond
surrounded by willows &—gold fish in it that long, Cousin
Sam. And I've got—you know—I've got a brewery! Pipes
leading to the house. Just turn on the fasset. Ah, ha, ha,
ha![45]

Keokuk, Ia., Jan 14, 1885.
It is near midnight, but I must send you a good-night
kiss. We were belated on the train by an ugly snowstorm

& I had to go upon the platform at 8 without having eaten since half past one. The house was full & though the audience had to be waked up, yet it became enthusiastic at length & we sent it away at 10/10 hungry for more. . . .

Burlington, Ia. Jan 15, 1885.

. . . We had to rise at four this morning to take the cars. Reached here at 7 less a quarter, and put up at the poorest hotel I have seen in all my northern or western travels.

Mark is not with us—has lingered in Keokuk to see his aged mother & will get here only tonight just before or after the beginning of the reading.

I am pressed by the Century editors for the work I promised them & which I have not yet been able to complete. . . .

Chicago, Jan 17, 1885.

I want to write you a long letter but I cannot. Twice today I must be on the platform & the time is near at hand. I am so hurried that I can think of nothing to say. Am trying to complete that Century paper "The Fall of New Orleans," with the editors prodding me. . . .[46]

Chicago, Jan 17, 1885.

. . . We have just finished our last reading in Chicago; one of the greatest successes, if not the very greatest, artistic and pecuniary success of our season. The thermometer is 4° below zero and falling. The snow crunches and rings as though it were some powdered metal.

Ah! what an effect we did have tonight. Clemens's story of Huck Finn & Tom Sawyer liberating runaway

[Jim] was received with a continual tempest of merriment, and when I gave "A Sound of Drums" I saw persons in tears all over the house. I was called back twice after my Creole songs and twice after "Mary's Night Ride." Mark & I both seemed especially inspired tonight & to inspire each other. A lady far back in the audience waved her handkerchief to me. I couldn't make out that I knew her at all. The same thing happened in almost exactly the same way in Toronto.

The matinée, today, too, was delightful. Among those who came into the retiring room were an old gentleman and lady who introduced themselves as Mr. & Mrs. Hammond. The lady was a sister of Owen Lovejoy, the Alton martyr.[47] The old gentleman began—"Mr. Cable I came to thank you for your paper on the Freedman"—and there choked, burst into tears and could not speak. His wife tried & made the same failure.

I wish you could see my table—covered with letters full of tender expressions of gratitude and admiration from white men & black men. That paper is turning out to be the greatest thing I've ever done.

Yesterday I had three interviewers at once hearing me on that subject. . . .

Let me see; I have not told you about our evening at Burlington, Iowa. Clemens lingered behind at Keokuk to see his aged mother—from whose fine aged face he gets all his own best lines—and was to reach Burlington just in time for the reading. But the snow storm was tremendous, his train was dreadfully belated and I had to lift a stone-dead audience out of the grave, as it were, and put life & mirth into them & keep their spirits rising for an hour & a half all alone. I did it, however, & when Clemens came

into the house at 9/35 my work was much more than done
& he had an enthusiasm to start on. I was proud of the
job. . . .

P. S. I keep forgetting to tell you that as we were about
to cross St. Louis bridge last week, two cars, the one in
front of ours & our own left the track. The one in front
was turned quite awry & for an instant there was a panic
but no one was hurt. I rose but did not leave my seat.[48]

Janesville, Wis. Jan 20, 1885.

At length my paper for the Century is done & goes into
[the] same mail with this.[49] Now you shall have longer
letters. Arrived here at 1/30 P.M. from Chicago. Snow,
snow, snow! But clear skies overhead and sweet sunshine.
So let it be in your heart.

Now I must be off to bed so as to be fresh tonight. My
health & strength need give you no concern. I weigh 111
pounds. . . .[50]

Madison, Wis., Jan 21, 1885.

It is midnight. We cannot go to bed. We must take a
train after one o'clock tonight & travel until 9 o'clock
tomorrow to reach LaCrosse. We read tonight to a packed
house. It was one of the most perfect evenings we have
ever had.

I can't write. Mark Twain is telling California yarns
to Ozias and Karl Strakasch. . . .

Minneapolis, Jan 24/85.

Once more I have the chance to write on programmes.
Mark's publisher has been using the backs to advertise
"Huck Finn" but we've shut him off now.

I am just off the stage after my 1st number. The opera house is beautiful, & full to the ceiling with an eager audience—the most eager to start with that we've ever had. Laughter & applause has begun from the very start. . . .

Winona, Minn., Jan 26, 1885.

What was my joy this evening when a letter from Major Pond to Ozias told us we should be in Albany on the 20th of Feb'y! . . .

. . . We must rise at 5 tomorrow morning to take cars. O how home-sick I am. . . .

Madison Wis. Jan 28/85.

Off again. Forward to Milwaukee. Ozias has been badly damaged by our hard journeying in a rigorous climate & will have to leave us, or rather be left by us there. I have telegraphed Major Pond to come on at once; which I do not suppose he can do. He will send some one else, no doubt. Poor Ozias! His heart & lungs are both in a sad condition. He was far from sound when we started out last November.

Clemens & I keep in perfect health. We called on ex-Gov. Fairchild[51] & family yesterday, found them sitting down to midday luncheon & ate with them. . . .

Milwaukee, Jan 29, 1885.

The days creep slowly by. . . .

I have been all day, nearly, nursing Ozias. He got very ill on arriving here and is already replaced by another manager. Poor fellow! he has been so brave & has suffered so much, & though I feel I was tardy in taking him in hand yet I am glad I was the first to speak. . . .

Tomorrow I have to leave him. We go to Rockford, Illinois. We had not a small audience—but a big auditorium & a poorly filled one. But we sent away the people so pleased that tonight the house seems almost full below & above. Well, well, what a profound impression my Freedman paper has made. Men come & say "we are Democrats, but you have told everything so plainly & convincingly that we see the whole thing in a new light." And they come & continue to come. Two newspapers interviewed me on the subject today. . . .

I have just come off the platform after reading "A Sound of Drums." Don't think I ever read it quite so well & there seemed to be a profound effect; but somehow it didn't show itself in applause to the extent I thought it would. At least I was not called back. But indeed I don't often get the 1st encore; that generally falls to Mark; but once they begin they keep it up right through.

Mark is on one of his best things now—marked * on the back of this [the "King Sollermun" selection from *Huckleberry Finn*] & will surely be called back. I hear the ladies laughing at the tops of their voices, & whenever they do that the encore is certain to come.

I write these trivialities because it seems like having you by & because I suppose it makes you feel so.

Now here is the strangest thing! A house full of people, seemingly highly entertained but feeble in their final applauses. Mark was not called back & I, following, was so feebly encored that I did not feel justified in doing more than bowing. Fact is Mark is under a cloud tonight

—feels it, confesses it, but cannot explain it. He doesn't take hold of his hearers and swing them as usual. There! he gets it at last. Even now it came as a kind of after thought from the audience after they had entirely ceased clapping. But it came good and heartily.

Strongest, heartiest kind of a reception to "Mary's Ride." Now Mark is on to finish; but I know he is going to come off wringing his hands with vexation. Fact is our hard railroad travel is telling on us—has let out—slackened—our nerves. Queerly, but truly, we feel it most after a partial resting spell. I am not feeling it much tonight & I think it is because I have been so busy all day. Mark has done nothing and is knocked up. The clock strikes ten. The end is only a few moments away. *Finis*. Mark explains it all. He had a *warm bath* ½ an hour before the reading. He'll never take another. . . .

Rockford Ill. Jan 30, 1885.
Well, it's queer. Here we come wandering into a town nobody ever heard of & into a poor stove-heated "hotel" with "banged" girls hovering over you & reciting the bill of fare in the dining room & serving dinner on a red table cloth; and yet when we come to our platform work here is the darlingest little "opera house," a beautifully appointed stage, and an auditorium & balconies full of a high style of audience. I have not seen so many bright & so many pretty faces looking toward the footlights since last Saturday.

I am reminded by something Mark is saying, of what a fine instinctive art he has for the platform. He has worked & worked incessantly on these programmes until he has effected in all of them—there are 3—a gradual growth of both interest & humor so that the audience never has to find anything less, but always more, entertaining than what precedes it. He says "I don't want them to get tired out laughing before we get to the end." The result is we have always a steady crescendo ending in a double climax. My insight into his careful, untiring, incessant labors are an education almost as valuable as that got from Sargent & Henderson. There! It does me good to hear them call him back at the place where the encores generally begin, instead of letting him go as they did in Milwaukee last night. Goodbye. I sang badly tonight. They encored me, but they hadn't ort to a-done it. . . .

Davenport, Ia, Jan 31, 1885.

. . . I don't expect my wife to take it blithly when my slanderers are howling at my heels. But don't forget that men who speak boldly for the truth must have slanderers no matter where they live, North, South, East, West. . . .

Had a strange experience this morning. Crossed the Mississippi on the snow-covered ice in a sleigh. Walked part of the distance. The whole drive from shore to shore was nearly a mile—not being straight across, but aslant.

Go down to New Orleans? Yes, I should like greatly to go. I should then have a chance to find out who are my friends and who are not. But I must admit I shall not from choice bring up my daughters in that state of society. The more carefully I study it the less I expect of it; and though there is no reason why I should indulge ungracious feelings toward it I cannot admire it or want my children to be brought up under its influence. . . .

In more than one of her letters Cable's wife remarked on the attacks that were being leveled at him, particularly in the Southern press.

Davenport, Ia., Jan 31, 1885.

I shall merely begin this letter now to finish it tomorrow. What a superb time we had tonight in the opera-house! Both Mark & I were in superb trim and the house was full of extremely bright people from parquet to pit. Mark was called back three times after his "Trying Situation" & I was called three times after "Mary's Night Ride." The little lady who came to show me her *Smerinthus Cablei*[52] told me that the women were sobbing all around her during the reading.

How much good a little attention to the body does. We had a hard night of it. Took a passenger coach on the end of a freight train at eleven, (the train kept back an *hour* & furnished with the coach, for our special convenience, by the superintendent, who came to see us off) changed cars (trains) into a sleeper, at Davis Junction, at 12/15 A.M., changed again into another train & sleeper at 3/45 at "Savanna," were wakened at 7 o'clock, took the sleigh trip through the snow & across the Mississippi that I told you of, got breakfast here, wrote letters (Mark & Adams played billiards), received Miss Sanders's call at 12/30 P.M., dined at 1/15, read till 2/30, went to bed, slept till nearly 6, supped lightly & felt ready for anything. Found Clemens heavy as lead—all unstrung. Advised a cup of black coffee. He took it, braced up in a moment, & we had as nearly perfect an entertainment as we have ever produced. . . .

Chicago, Feb'y 3, 1885.

I can't write much today. Had a hard trip yesterday & made it harder by writing on the cars and talking to persons who made themselves acquainted. Read here last night. Was tired, heavy and depressed by news of a sick wife in Simsbury. "Mary's Night Ride" went without an encore—partly my fault, I think, & partly the result of earlier encores being refused. . . .

Feb 3, 1885.

To O. W. Pond
   Plankinton House
    Milwaukee:

Now wit you well, Sir Sagramore, thou good knight and gentle, that there be two that right wonderly do love thee, grieving passing sore and making great dole at thy heavy travail. And we will well that thou prosper at the hand of the leech, and come lightly forth of thy hurts, and be as thou were tofore.

     Sir Mark Twain. Sir Geo. W. Cable.

Sweet wife: I send you, above, a copy of a telegram sent last night after midnight to Ozias by Mark & [me]. We enjoyed it so much ourselves that I made a copy for each of our wives. I can't write today. So many things to do & travel besides. Major Pond has reached us. . . .

Chicago, Feb'y 3, 1885.

Here's a blank programme-back. Very pleasant indeed it is to write tonight, for there is a vast audience in the house rising tier upon tier from pit to dome to tell us goodbye. Mark's very first number was encored. I followed as you will see (other side) with "A Sound of Drums." Every word of it came from the bottom of my heart, I was in superb voice, and they called me back. They wouldn't take a mere bow & I sang "Brave Boys" to loud applause. Mark is telling one of his very best numbers & the old surf-roar is booming. They will encore every number to the end.

Ah! what a noble applause calls Mark back, continuing until he has returned entirely back across the broad platform to the footlights.

Funny thing just now. I had been out & sung two Creole songs & on retiring the applause died down & Mark in his nervous way stepping out on the platform a little too promptly was met by a pattering encore intended for the singer. It was awkward for him, but he was equal to the emergency. He stood still a moment, then said in the drollest way imaginable—"I'll go back and get him"— At which there was a roar of laughter & applause in the midst of which he came back to make his word good. Of course I would not go, so he went back and raised another laugh, saying, "He's sung all he knows"—and went on with "The Jumping Frog," which is getting a superb reception.

Well, my work is done. "Mary's Night Ride" was encored all right & I sang "Salangudou." Mark is finishing. What a fine night it has been. . . .

Lafayette, Ind. Feb'y 6, 1885.

. . . Last night & the night before we were in Indiana; South Bend & Fort Wayne—ah! the dreary, dismal taverns, and dingy, dirty platforms & auditoriums. Mark says, "Once more we resume a dog's life." I reply, "Worse than that;—two dogs' lives." Yet the audiences are bright & hearty & half the fault lies in us because we are spoiled by our city experiences. From a Chicago audience of 1600 people to South Bend with—say 350 people is not cheerful. And the early rising, and the fiendish stove heat, & dirty hacks and drafty railway cars smelling of coal furnaces and human-kind—well, well! I'm growling!

But my nose is running like two Minnehahas and my nose is growing red. . . .

Indianapolis, Feb 8, 1885.

It is nearly 11 o'clock Sabbath night and only now have I the chance to write you a few lines. I have had a most delightful day. I had a hard struggle yesterday to keep from being sick, and yet had two readings to do besides the travel from Lafayette, involving early rising & other discomforts.

In the matinée I had a hard time and did what I, at least, knew to be poor work; & yet I had one pleasure; for, for the first time in my life, I heard an applause follow me off the platform that was entirely the clapping of ladies' hands. I never saw men so scarce in an audience before. The sound was very sweet to the ear of a weary, brainsick man.

At night I feared I should not get through the performance at all; but, bless you, I hadn't been on the platform 2 minutes before I saw I was going to do the very best work; & in fact did render Raoul's two scenes (in *The Grandissimes*) better than I'd ever done them before in my life. As to Mary's Ride the applause was tremendous. I saw one lady in the middle of the house sit & cry all through it.

98

After the reading I felt so well that Mark & I went to a reception. . . .

. . . They tell me the V. Pres/t was in our audience when we were here a few weeks ago. . . .[53]

After service went in with Dr. McLeod to his residence next door. . . . Had a bright half hour with them & so back to the hotel & entrapped Mark into a discussion of the duty of practicing religion—from his point of view— whipped him off the field & left him, he saying as I went he wished he had gone to church with me. Would to God I might prevail to take him there. Help me with your prayers, beloved. . . .

Columbus Ohio, Feb 9, 1885.

Got here only an hour before the time to read, having traveled since 10/45 this morning. Have been writing hard all day on the cars, amending the latter part of my paper on "The Fall of New Orleans." A ton of correspondence has tumbled upon me again and on top of that the call to write a reply to the article of Mr. Grady of the Atlanta *Constitution* attacking my "Freedman's Case in Equity."[54] There is little chance for me to rest & I may have to send telegrams to you instead of writing letters, except when I can do it this way, on programs. . . .

We are having a full house & a tremendous time tonight although it has rained & stormed all day & is spitting snow tonight. Albany is uncertain again; we may get in there & we may fail, the trouble is to find a suitable hall not engaged for that particular night.

The reception of our little show is immense tonight. It is like Toronto, Detroit &c. The audience is one of the most cultivated in appearance that I have ever seen out of a great city. I have only my last number to do & then I must go to an hour's hard work to mail my MS to the Century eds. . . .

Columbus, O. Feb'y 10, 1885.

No further letter today except to say that I wrote last night till 1/30 A.M., retired, woke at 9 A.M. & am well & cheerful & strong & happy & have mailed my MS. . . .

Delaware, O, Feb 10, 1885.

Once more I turn to this sweet task. We are in an inland town again; but before what a bright audience!

I had a good time today. Went to see Gov. Hoadly.[55] He was ever so cordial. We drew up chairs & sat around the fire, he, his sect'y, the Att'y Gen'l (if I understood aright) and I. He is, you know, one of the national leaders of the Democracy; and yet he hastened to say at once that he knew my utterances on the Freedman question & was with me entirely. It was, to me, one of the most comforting & encouraging hours I have spent in many a long day.

Later, he came to see us, Mark & [me], but mainly, I think, Mark; & we spent another pleasant time. He gave me several points to use against my Bourbon friends down in Louisiana & Georgia.

I have been on the stage twice, now, & have only twice more to go to have done for tonight. Am learning something every evening & think I did better tonight in Ristofalo's Courtship than ever before.

It is bitter cold again; 13° below zero & falling. We are rejoicing with all our powers that tomorrow night is the last that finds us in a town. Nothing but cities there-after. . . .

En route, between Oberlin & Detroit.
Feb. 12, 1885.

I have had poor chance to write since my last. We had to take cars three times yesterday & wait in and about little stove-heated way-stations, for belated trains. The whole day was taken up in going about 100 miles. The themometer started at 24° below zero, but climbed up nearly to the zero point. We reached Oberlin at a quarter to seven and were to go upon the platform at *seven*. I did get on the platform at 7/20 & even then was inconvenienced by the tardy incoming of a special train from another town, that brought about a hundred auditors.

Strange to say I went to the work fresh & bright & from the very start did, by verdict of all, the finest evening's reading thus far in my experience. The very first number, that generally goes to make me acquainted & set the people a-smiling, was met with almost boisterous delight from the very start.

Clemens, on the contrary, found himself as heavy as lead—I mean in his own consciousness, and although the audience showed some heartiness of appreciation while he was before them, yet he came off disheartened, vexed, & full of lamentations over his condition.

On my 2d number I instantly shot ahead of any rendering I have ever before made of it. I was full of new inspirations, was interrupted early with applause, and when I came to where Ristofalo puts his arm around Kate they would not let me go any farther but drowned in applause my repeated efforts to proceed & when I finally got the better of them & went on, it was, so to speak, through breakers of laughter and applause, to the end, which was, however, just at hand.

Clemens met me behind the door with pantomimic expressions of amazement & was about to go on for his turn, when a rush of applause called me back. I went, but excused myself in an impromptu remark or two, as I wanted Mark to get back & redeem himself without delay & knew he was nearly sick to do so. As I came off once more I saw intense gratification in his face.—"That was most gracefully said," he exclaimed, and went out on the platform.

But still he rolled in the trough of the sea. The audience was greatly pleased—full of laughter; but I knew, even by their limited demonstration & he knew most painfully that he was way below par. However, he was called back, told his drollest yarn, and captured them at last. But if I had been in bad condition, too, we should have had the dreariest night of the season.

My songs were encored—There, now, I believe I'm wrong; I think Mark was not called back until after his 3d piece. He felt his deficiency the more distressingly because the previous night he had been nearly as bad. However it was, he began at length to rally. In "Mary's Night Ride" I introduced some improvements that had occurred to me the night before while hearing General Homer Pond—another brother of the Major—tell about a perilous ride of his under fire. The effect was great.

In the midst of the story a comical thing occurred. At the point where the negro guide speaks his loud whispered goodbye to Mary & the spy, saying "I feared you gwine fo'git it, boss," in the midst of the death-like stillness which always reigns throughout the house just then, a black man, sitting behind me in a sort of choir loft all alone & in sight of every one, recognized the mimicked African enunciation and the old southern title of respect, let go a suppressed but loud titter of the purest Ethiopian character, and its character as well as its irrelevancy brought down the house. Yet it rather helped than hindered me, and when I came to the fierce thrilling end I knew by every symptom, both inward & outward, that I had done the best bit of reading I had ever done in my life.

In response to the encore I excused myself—Mark *never* objects to my declining an encore—& read a little note that had come in while Mark was on the platform, asking him to read the story of the "Golden Arm." So then out he came and read it & did it well & was called back & did another thing and did it his very best & so the evening ended, and presently the retiring room was full of new friends.

The audience was large—filled the house—& was one of the brightest I ever saw. . . .[56]

Tonight we read in Detroit against fearful odds, to wit, the Governor's *levée.*

Well, goodbye. Here's a long letter, such as men choose their wives to victimize with because no one else would tolerate their long & flattering accounts of themselves. But I make believe you like it, & you're afraid to say you don't.

Goodbye, I tell you! How many times—

After all, we are not to read in Albany, but in Saratoga & must take cars at once for New York as soon as the reading is over. But on the Monday following we read in N. Haven. . . .

Detroit, Feb 12, 1885.

Why have you not acknowledged receipt of two photographs made in Quincy, Illinois, one a cabinet of myself & the other a group with Clemens on one extreme & me on the other & a gentleman & 3 ladies between? ...

Detroit, Feb 12, 1885.

I shall not talk about the performance tonight. I gave you enough of that last night. Only I may say that we are agreeably surprised to find the house quite full tonight notwithstanding the Governor's *levée*. I don't feel bright tonight. The long hard railroad work is beginning to come back upon me in a relaxing condition & a loss of brilliancy in voice and spirit. I don't like this programme. It is too uncertain in its effects; sometimes very good & sometimes poor. ...

Well, I *will* talk about the programme; for I've got to say it's my turn tonight. I'm going all to pieces. Have read two numbers & don't get hold of the audience with any force at all. Dear, dear! how dreadful the feeling is! Especially when one knows, sees & feels that the fault is not in the audience at all but in the utter looseness and softness—flabbiness of all his energies. O me! I've got to go out there presently and sing.

Well, I'm through! The audience gave me the usual responsive calls & so I am not desolate; but I am still left with the knowledge that I didn't do nearly my best. ...

London, Ont. Feb 13, 1885.

... We're in a Y.M.C.A. hall tonight, a pretty little one, with a small, bright audience, that seems to have very little knowledge of us but is very willing to learn. My

first piece, just finished, was unusually successful. I am
full of spirit tonight; it is much like the Y.M.C.A. night
in New York; little impromptu things pop out of my
mouth before I know it and bring down the house.

O, dear, dear, dear; must I forever talk about this platform work? But when I'm at it I can't think of much else
& I know if I just clatter along you will like it better than
blank paper. . . .

Goodnight. Pleasant dreams. The jovial Pond answers
my question—"Where do you suppose this town gets such
pretty hydrant water as it has?"—"From Canada. All
these towns along here get their water from Canada." . . .

Toronto Feb'y 15, 1885.

. . . As we were leaving the hall on Friday evening in
London, we encountered a large group of young seminary
girls in charge of a lady teacher who introduced herself &
invited us to visit the school a little way out of town. A
moment later the principal, a Mr. English, repeated the
invitation urgently and proposed to call for us next morning at 8/45 with a sleigh. We accepted.

The morning drive was one of the most delightful I
have ever had in my whole life. The thermometer had
been 21 below zero in the night & was still below. The sun
shone bright and clear over dazzling hills and still, white
valleys. The distances were half veiled in a tender opaline
haze. The deep snowdrifts lay in long, graceful curling
billows like foamless breakers turned to white marble.
The tinkle of sleigh bells was everywhere. The snow
creaked under the flying runners, the frost hung from the
horses' muzzles, breasts and flanks, men's beards hung

hard & heavy and white with ice, and the still air was pure, cold and sweet like the waters of a crystal spring.

The school—Helmuth Female College—stood upon a high hill with its grounds undulating away on every hand in spotless white. Soon we were out of the sleigh robes, and free of our wraps and overwear, seated among a group of teachers male & female, sipping good coffee from blue china.

Presently we went down a stair and into the drawing rooms. Mark and I are certainly a pair of hardened old tramps, but it as surely taxed our power of face to the utmost to enter & stand in silence before that ranged battery of seventy-odd pairs of young girls' eyes. I can only say we did not run or crawl under the furniture.

Then the presentation began. The girls were brought forward by twos and introduced by the principal first to me and then to Clemens, that happening to be the order in which we had entered and were standing. Fortunately the place each girl was from was mentioned and so I had frequent opportunity to say a short, pleasant word about their various homes—which, oddly enough, were mostly in the States. At length this pleasant labor was done. Then came the autograph books and every girl in the school, and the teachers, too, asked an autograph. Clemens sat at a round table in one parlor & I at another in the other parlor and the work began. I dated all mine "St. Valentine's Day, 1885" adding now & then the words of some lucky thought, and indulging once in a while in some conversational fencing with some of the teachers.

This over the cry was for the toboggans. Away went the girls for furs and like belongings and out we sallied with them, walking, laughing, skipping along the beaten path and some of them, trying to make short cuts over the snow-crust, breaking through and tumbling headlong, but up again and on with rosy cheeks and snow-dusted robes and laughter and shouts and every boisterous innocence. So to the crest of a precipitate hill that ran off below into a broad level field whose snow crust was unbroken. A moment of preparation, a piling on of girls and then away we went! The toboggan that I was on went, on its second trip down, far beyond any other. When it finally came to a stand and we got off to toil back it was through snow more than knee deep. We were long recovering the top of the hill and as, with laugh & shout, we did so it was to find it deserted & to be told that a telephone message had been received stating that a change had been made in the movement of trains and that the train for Toronto was at the moment being held for us at the London station.

Clemens was already gone. I saw him in a pretty sleigh behind a tandem team whisking through the distant gate of the grounds and those seventy girls waving and hurrahing and he swinging his hat and tossing kisses right and left; and the scene repeated again as he swept around the slope of a hill & came in sight again a few hundred yards farther on.

In a moment I was in another sleigh drawn by two horses abreast, a young lady, one of the teachers, an extremely pretty woman, by the way, was in beside me; the huge furs were bundled around and off we flew, down through the cheering, waving lane of pretty maids, out into the road, into view again, waving, throwing kisses, laughing, cheering, the horses clattering at full gallop and the snowing road gliding under us.

We missed the train by a few minutes; its conductor

could get no telephonic reply that we were coming, and after waiting 25 minutes departed.

We arrived here by a later train, after dark. We dressed in haste, went to the hall, & read to a thin audience. It is rather humiliating to see a house dotted noticeably with empty seats when we had looked for a crowded house.

This morning woke so late that I had to dispense with breakfast in order to get to church in time. . . .

Brockville, Canada, Feb 16, 1885.

On the platform again. From hotel to hotel our journey today was a matter of eleven hours in a passenger coach. Snow pouring down all day long piling up, up, up. The storm roaring & blustering, the train losing time steadily, now and then making long, weary stops in the snow until the snow plow running on in advance should clear the way. Waiting once for a train ahead, of five cars, all of them off the track, to get back on the rails and out of our way. . . .

Ottawa, Feb'y 17, 1885.

Hard railroading must make short letters. We have seen a Canadian snowstorm of full stature. Trains blocked by the snow & in one case that I saw, three locomotives required to pull out one train—passenger train. . . .

We did not read in Kingston. The appointment was changed to Brockville & I shall not get my Kingston mail till tomorrow in Montreal. . . .

Montreal Feb'y 19, 1885.

Put Montreal down as one of the brightest, liveliest and most charming cities—at least in winter—that can be. We got here something after noon of yesterday. I can't tell you of all the pretty sights. There is much quaint old, and not a little good new, architecture. The snow is wonderful to see, for quantity and for beauty. The remains of the Carnival, i.e. the statuary of ice and the ice-palace (it should be ice-castle) are extremely fine. I don't describe them, there is no time for that. The dress of the Canadian people is picturesque beyond anything else in America. The furs, in endless quantity, and variety of kind and color, are enough to give most striking character to them without anything further; but to this feature is added the frequent costumes of the snowshoers & tobogganers (or tobogganists if that is it) white, red, blue, brown and other flannels in solid colors and tasteful bands & facings of one color on another, and the sashes & belts & hoods and moccasins. It is a charming sight. And the superb sleighs with their wealth of fur robes, and their elegant teams and tinkling bells; and the rosy cheeks & hurried steps. One cannot describe these things. The people have simply turned the bitter months of the year into days so full of exhilaration that there is hardly left time for sleep.

We dined at one & went to bed. Slept till 4/30 and then went into the hotel's three large drawing-rooms thrown into one, where the Athenaeum Club were to give us a grand reception. It lasted till six and was the most elaborate affair I have ever had part in. I don't think I could have shaken less than two hundred and fifty hands. Mark Twain & I were not required to stand together and in one or two other ways there was an air of ease given to the whole matter. From first to last I enjoyed it greatly. Major Pond tells me he has sent you a paper with an account of it, but I enclose a clipping from the same paper, a copy which he handed me.

In the evening we read to a huge audience full of enthusiasm and yet critical; a peculiar and specially pleasing audience—something like Toronto's & something like Boston's.

After the reading we went, by starlight, at headlong speed, bundled in furs to the eyes, in a sleigh, through & out of the town up, up, over the hills looking down upon the twinkling city as upon a brooch of innumerable topazes and diamonds, on and on with the Great Bear almost directly overhead and the creaking, groaning snow underfoot, the new moon not long set and the horses' bells jingling in our front, until we drew up at last at a door by the wayside where a large man in a snowshoer's uniform bade us welcome and helped us to alight.

Up a stair and into a room blue with the smoke of innumerable pipes & cigars, our ears deafened with the wild cheers of uniformed snowshoers—the "Toute Bleue" club, huzzaing at our—I doubt not I should say Mark Twain's —entrance. So we were walked down the middle of the room to the platform at the bottom; but just as we set foot on its lowest step, the master of ceremonies called for silence and formally announced our arrival & presence, and proposed that as Mark Twain was already a member of the club though never seen by them before, he should be initiated. Instantly, with a roaring cheer he was laid hold of and walked out into the middle of the floor. Then at the word "Bounce um!" he was lifted from his feet in the midst of a tightly huddled mass of young athletes, laid out at full length on their hands and then—what think you?—thrown bodily into the air almost to the ceiling, caught upon their hands as he came down, thrown up again, caught again, thrown again—so four, five times amid resounding cheers.

Then the cry was for me. It was my turn. The sensation, you may imagine, was something tremendous. To know that one is falling horizontally back downward, through the impalpable air, depending on a lot of young snow-shoers to catch him & throw him up again, is something that must be experienced to be—enjoyed.

Well, then Mark was walked up upon the platform for a speech which he made with great effect. Then I, & I am still enjoying the satisfaction of having been extremely fortunate in my expressions, being greeted with laughter at every period.

Then, if you'll believe me, they "bounced" the gigantic Major Pond. It was a sight to see that huge, black bundle of wraps go up to the ceiling & back & up again & back again.

Got to stop.

Evening.

Today I found I was taxing my best forces by writing & had to stop short. Now, here behind the platform, I shall resume. . . .

After our speeches a song was sung. At every point where a speech or song was to be given the word was first "sit down," and it was a bright—a charming sight, to see that great hall full of jolly fellows in their white & blue flannel uniforms with tasseled hoods falling down the back sink to floor and sit cross-legged upon their buskins & moccasins. Then I was hauled out for a song & gave them Zizi, they taking up the chorus. Then an anecdote—one of his inimitable "yarns"—from Clemens, a little speech of one sentence—but good—from Pond, a jolly snowshoe song & chorus, really very pretty; and then those superb young stalwarts sang—it was a grand sight— sang "God Save the Queen."

There were many pleasant features that I cannot take time to tell about. They had a fashion of applauding— smiting the hands together with a single deafening clap, letting an interval of nearly a second pass by, then giving another, then another, then another, shortening the interval of silence gradually until they broke into a storm of sound thus—[intervals indicated].

We drove home at a gallop—it is common to see horses dragging sleighs at that pace. I shall not try to describe a sleigh ride in the starlight! We took supper at twelve and retired near one.

I woke at half past nine, breakfasted & went out sleigh-riding with Pond & Mr. Iles (I can't spell his name but he is the prince of hotel keepers). We visited two or three quaint old churches & then went to a toboggan slide. Pond & I went down together. It is like being shot out of a cannon. We went, easily, a quarter of a mile along the level snow after darting down the hill. The descent is on snow that has been wetted & turned into glare ice. It is tremendous sport & looks frightful; but ladies & children indulge in it constantly.

Came back to the hotel, slept—for these experiences make great drafts on the nerves & at 3 o'clock waked & received Dr. Louis Frechette, whose name you may remember—the Canadian poet. He has translated some of my stories into French. He staid quite a long time though a pleasant one, & then I dressed, dined, wrote & came here to this show.

Have now finished my part of the programme & answered my encore, singing badly tonight, I don't know why for I read my very best.

Tomorrow we leave Canada and read tomorrow night in Saratoga.

Back in the hotel. From the hall we went to the toboggan slide of the "Toute Bleues" and took two of those leaps down through the air—for that is what they seem to be. And so goodbye to Canada. We expect a hard day tomorrow, for the snow is drifting & the railways will be choked. But delay is the worst we have to anticipate. . . .

NY, Feb 26, '85.

Had a great time in Newark last night; one of the finest nights we have had for some ten days. Orange was very poor—i.e. the audience was slim; which was a great surprise to us & not to be accounted for.

I can't write today; too busy; "write all time wasn't too busy." I shall probably not make that southern reading tour, but I am thinking of running down to N. Orleans from Washington next Monday and almost straight back again to Simsbury. . . .

Philadelphia Feb 27, 1885.

. . . I slept yesterday afternoon & last night Mark & I stood before an audience of about 3000 people in the beautiful Academy of Music here. It was the finest sight I have ever looked at from the platform. And I had great success. As to Mark his was not up to high water mark though—excuse me, the pun was accidental—he created much enthusiasm. I don't see what is the matter with him except that he seems tired out. . . .

Balt/o, Md. Feb 27, 1885.

I have about made up my mind to go South. Hope to be back by the 10th of March. We are reading now in a huge, ugly building called the Natatorium. It *is* a bathing school in summer, I believe. The audience is just one flat expanse of faces stretching away back until the faces become a confused mass. There is great enthusiasm. A narrow balcony runs around the sides and is full, of course, of people. The unsightly roof is made tolerable with festoons of evergreen.

Dear, dear! Mark is himself once more, and it's a great comfort. . . .

D. C. Feb'y 28, 1885.

I have your letter of 26 & 27, and know how bitterly you feel the disappointment of my turning southward instead of coming home. But pet, this is making my southern trip at the least objectionable time that I can make it at all, and making it shorter than it would be any other time. I do not go from choice. If I pleased myself I would take the first train for Simsbury. But I have a duty to do & you must help me do it. So must the children. . . .

D. C. Mar 2, 1885.

In an hour & a half I shall be off for New Orleans. . . .

Spent a long, good day yesterday with Carrie Henderson & her husband Lieut. Wadhams. Clemens was with us. I got him out to church at last! . . .

THE AFTERNOON
OF A FRIENDSHIP

Judged by any likely measure, the joint reading tour was successful. Though Mark Twain had written Charles L. Webster, the manager of his business affairs, that he would have made more money if he had stayed at home and written a book,[57] *the venture in fact had paid him well—something like $16,000 clear for the fifteen weeks on the road. Cable had been paid about $5,000 and Pond about $3,000. There had been echoing applause in almost every hall, and the newspaper reports had spread the fame of the readings to thousands who did not hear them. Moreover, the tour had served to call attention to their books, and in particular their latest,* Dr. Sevier *and* Huckleberry Finn. *There had been friction between Mark Twain and Pond once when Mark grew dissatisfied with the traveling managers and insisted that Pond come from New York and himself make the local arrangements. At one point Pond asked Cable to intercede with Mark Twain in the matter.*[58] *But Pond joined them for the last days of the tour and apparently relations were as cordial as ever. On the evidence of Cable's letters there had been only pleasantness between the two partners, and this evidence is supported by the fact that when the last reading had been given and they were ready to go separate ways, they spent an additional day together in Washington.*

In Mark Twain's mind, however, all was not smooth to the end of the tour. Cable and he both felt the strain and the monotony, and both were harassed by interests they could not manage adequately on the road. Some of the letters Mark Twain wrote his wife in the last weeks of the tour contain remarks extravagantly critical of Cable, and it is clear that Mark Twain was irritated during their last six weeks together, though his severest strictures often appear alongside his customary praise of Cable.[59] His warmest invectives were aimed at Cable's strict observance of the Sabbath. When the contracts for the tour were being drawn in the summer of 1884, Mark could make a joke of Cable's refusal to travel on Sunday; and in a much-quoted letter written to Howells after the tour had closed he said that traveling with Cable had taught him "to abhor and detest the Sabbath-day and hunt up new and troublesome ways to dishonor it." In the same letter he said of the tour: "It has taught me that Cable's gifts of mind are greater and higher than I had suspected."[60] In a statement such as he often made, Mark Twain wrote to his wife from Indianapolis on January 7, 1885, saying that Cable had "his littlenesses, like Napoleon," but that he was a "brave soul & a great man."

In a letter to Pond on December 22, during the Christmas holiday from the platform, Mark Twain lamented that with the encores the program had grown too long and vowed that Cable's time must be reduced. Cable should give only one encore, he said, and that after the popular "Mary's Night Ride," but he would himself continue to answer the usual encores. As a consequence a new plan was inaugurated, apparently with Cable's full ap-

proval, so that Cable, for one thing, would open the program sharply at eight rather than delay the customary ten minutes for the audience to assemble. In a letter to his wife Mark Twain explained the new plan and added, "And privately, another thing—only half the house hears C's first piece."[61] This remark and others which Mark Twain put into his letters home make it clear that in stating his irritation with his companion he was indulging in the kind of deliberate hyperbole which he and those around him enjoyed as regular fare. It seems to have been his habit to plant words or entire passages in what he was writing, as a game with his wife, inviting her protests when she read the manuscripts. His remarks on Cable probably were phrased in part with the same purpose in mind.

Mark Twain was tired in his last weeks on the road and was exasperated over the management of his many interests. He wrote Webster he hoped to get in a good humor again when the tour was over. It happened often that he was dissatisfied with his own performances, and often at times when his partner's success on the stage was greatest. Furthermore, Cable had become a celebrated man with the publication of "The Freedman's Case in Equity," so that in their last six weeks Mark saw himself not eclipsed but nearly equaled in popularity both on and off the platform. The wonder is perhaps not that Mark was irritated by Cable's habits of mind and conduct that were so different from his own, but rather that he exploded about Cable only a few times and then mainly to his wife. Mark Twain's comments to his wife and Pond were of course unknown to Cable, as were also any similar remarks he may have made to others. The letters Cable wrote during the tour contain not the slightest hint of any dissatisfaction with his companion. All the evidence is that he exulted in Mark's noble character, his fine artistic sense, and his success, and he was proud that he could hold his own with such a performer. He was pained when Mark was in the doldrums and rejoiced when he was at his best again. The tour came to an end with ostensibly good feelings all the way round. The fact that Mark Twain went to church with Cable in Washington on their last day together is apparent testimony that he had not actually resented Cable's earlier attempts to get him out to church.

On May 10, following the close of the tour, Mark Twain wrote Charles L. Webster, "From this on out, write nothing in any private letter to friend, relative, or anybody, which you do not want published. . . . Nobody is to be trusted. I have been burnt so often, in my own experiences that I feel like warning and saving you."[62] *His immediate concern was the delicate manipulation Webster then had in progress to secure publication rights to Ulysses S. Grant's memoirs. Yet this exhortation sounds a note reminiscent of the self-blame which was habitual with Mark Twain at embarrassing or painful moments in his life. Newspaper dispatches dealing with the reading tour seem to have provoked the confession.*[63]

The dispatches said that Cable, Mark Twain, and Pond had broken up with a quarrel and cited the grievances which each supposedly held against the others. The longest of the newspaper reports and the one containing the severest charges against Cable appeared on May 7 in the Boston *Herald, where Mark Twain would no doubt have seen it. A more generalized report on the affair was printed in the same paper on May 10, the day of Mark Twain's letter to Webster. In a telegram to Mark Twain on May 15 and a letter written the next day Cable declared that he had said nothing unfavorable about his companions of the reading tour and asked Mark to say whatever he might wish in the same regard. Mark Twain replied that he had not let "the slander of a professional newspaper liar" disturb him in the least and that it had not occurred to him to take notice of it in print. Prompted by a letter from Cable, the editor of the* Herald *sought an explanation from the New York correspondent who had originated the dispatch of May 7 and afterward printed a retraction and apology in his paper. Cable's friend Marion A. Baker in New Orleans asked why Mark Twain and Pond did not come forward and scotch all the rumors,⁶⁴ and since Mark Twain did not as a rule hesitate to set the newspapers right, he might have been expected to speak up. But neither he nor Pond had a word to say publicly.*

The assertions in the dispatch of May 7 were wide of the truth and many of them were patently absurd. Yet most of them had some relation to fact. And some of the facts could have come originally from no one but Mark Twain, as Cable realized and as Mark Twain could not fail to realize also. We can assume that Mark Twain was chagrined to realize that he was the source of slanders against one of his friends. It was in such a mood that he wrote to Webster on May 10.

The newspaper slanders may have produced a slight coolness, but apparently no real estrangement between Cable and Mark Twain. There was undoubted genuineness—and possibly a note of apology—in Mark's words to

Cable in 1895: "And I have always said, & still maintain, that as a railroad-comrade you were perfect—the only railroad-comrade in the world that a man of moods & frets & uncertainties of disposition could travel with, a third of a year, and never weary of his company."[65] For his part, Cable had showed from their first acquaintance an understanding of Mark Twain's nature and a generous tolerance of his habits. After their four months together he took any occasion that presented itself to pay public homage to Mark Twain as a great man and an esteemed friend; and apparently in no utterance, public or private, that has come down in any record did he disparage his friend in the slightest way.

At his home in Northampton, Massachusetts, Cable began in 1887 the Home Culture Clubs, which after a few years published The Letter, *a monthly magazine intended to report the activities of the several reading and study clubs for the benefit of the others. One of the sketches of contemporary authors Cable wrote for the magazine was on Mark Twain, in the issue of February 1, 1896.*

Samuel L. Clemens
"Mark Twain"

Fully nine-tenths of all the book reading done in the world is done for diversion rather than for education. We are entirely willing that our literature should inform and educate, but it *must* entertain us. At the same time, because reading is, or can be, one of the most useful delights in life, therefore, in order to the perfection both of its usefulness and its delight, we demand, that it shall not misinform or otherwise mislead us.

And besides: nowadays a great majority of us read

briefly. We read for rest, and for cheer; for rest after toil and trouble; for cheer in the midst of them. We take literature not as a locomotive devours coal and water, but a little at a time, as it takes oil on the road, and polishing in the round-house; or as a sailor takes his song, hauling the bowline. So it is that not the most informing books, but the most entertaining, not the richest in other men's thoughts but the richest in reminders of our own emotional experiences; not the most exact in art, but the most redolent of nature; and not the books that cannot be laid down, once we take them up, but the books that can be laid down and taken up again and again and again— these are the writings whose authors' names become and remain household words from palace to hut and from generation to generation. And such are Mark Twain's.

The test of a humor's quality is not the loudness or length of our laugh; that is the measure of its quantity. The test of its quality is the number of times we can part from and return to it and still find it amusing. But equally by both these tests, of quantity and quality, is Mark Twain beyond compare the greatest humorist in America, and one of the greatest in the world's literature. It is a credit to the genuine modesty of his character and the energy of his literary conscience and ambition, that he should be so earnestly desirous (as it is well known he is) not to be famous merely as a humorist. No man ever had an idler solicitude; a solicitude that could scarcely be more out of place in the breast of Cervantes. A humor like his is never mere humor nor mere nature; it is wisdom and truth and art as well. If it were not wise and true as well as 'funny' none of us would read it a record, seventh and seventieth time, while as for its art, few writers have ever disguised so much subtle art under such cunning ostentation of awkwardness. For "The Prince and the Pauper," and other works written with the same motive, the reading world will always rightly be grateful; but the only thing these triumphs prove which was not proved before are literary technique and versatility, of all things the two least worth proving. And yet, after all, it was good to have them proved.

But look at "The Innocents Abroad"! I do not say re-read it; simply look at the size, and then at the sale of it. Except the authors of Don Quixote and Pickwick Papers —and we must remember the Pickwick Papers were first issued in installments—I do not know if any writer has ever successfully dared to put forth so corpulent a volume supremely dedicated to laughter. It takes more to make a great humorist—it means more to be one—than we probably realize one time in a hundred; more, I venture to say, than the great humorist himself ever finds out.

To speak of the personal characteristics of Mr. Clemens would be a grateful task. But there is here no opportunity. I have but paid a moment's tribute to his genius and the poor space I had has given out. I can only hope for an-other time.

G. W. Cable.

At the dinner in New York celebrating Mark Twain's seventieth birthday, Cable was one of those who rose to pay his respects.[66]

Mr. Chairman, one hardly knows whether to be more elated or more terrified at such an opportunity as you have given me. I would I had the time to command my energies

which would have given me the assurance to come, as
some have come this evening, trusting to the inspiration
of the hour and the inspiration behind it of the man. I
have a lifetime's affection for Mark Twain, but my embarrassment consists in the fact that I come to you tonight with my strength discounted by a late sickness.
That I only mention in order that I, too, may have my
boast, that I have come from afar, nearly as far as Mr.
Carnegie, to pay my tribute to our loved friend. But I
must try and keep my head until I come to my manuscripts, and not be like that good man whom we heard on
the levee, Mark Twain, at New Orleans, when you came
there, and Uncle Remus and Osgood were with us, and
you read Bre'r Rabbit because we could not make Bre'r
Rabbit read his own piece; and when you were leaving
on the steamer every one was wanting to shake hands
with you, as every one wants to shake hands with you
wherever you go. And this good man was so full of the
elation of the moment, so intoxicated with the pure
spiritual joy of at least calling you by your best name or
pet name, that he had not sobered up quite even after
we were all pushed off the steamer, leaving you to go
up the river, and he was coming down the stage plank
with his arm around his friend's neck, saying—hardly
anything, but, "I, I was so embarrassed—I—I've read
everything he ever wrote, and I would thank him for
every one of them, and when I got hold of his hand my
heart was so big that the only thing I could think of his
to thank him for was the 'Heathen Chinee.'" (Laughter.)
So I hope that I may have said—I don't know what I
have said myself, but I hope it's all right, as I am assured
it is on my right hand,—but I was casting around for

some word of tribute that might be more especially my own to a friend whose threescore years and ten we are celebrating to-night, and I believe that I am the only one in this entire company who ever spent threescore and ten almost consecutive days of travel, alternating on the platform in partnership and companionship with Mark Twain. It may be, while our attention is still concentrated on our friend, there may be room for me to allude to him as the only accepted interpreter of his own pieces by word of mouth, and the charm of that interpretation doubtless every one here can testify to from his own experience, and it is quite enough for me to mention them for your loving contemplation without another word. Always there was inspired in his hearers, as in his readers, the perception that what he received came from a treasury which nothing could diminish. I count that experience in the years 1884 and 1885 as one of the most notable in my life. Just twenty-one years ago that was. Both of us looked that much younger; I had just turned forty years of age and I had reached the very crossing, as I thought, of the dividing line; one day my senior partner—the star in the troupe of two—remarked that he was passing his forty-ninth year. "Your seventh seven," I said, and he said, "My seventh seven"; and now he comes to his tenth seven, and I trust he will go on to the eleventh, the thirteenth, the fifteenth seven. (Applause.) I called that season one of the most notable in my life, because, for one thing, I saw underlying the homage of the people's heart all poured out in floods of affectionate embarrassment to the man on whom they looked with such esteem and whom they crowned the King of Mirth. I learned then the power of his marvelous and overwhelming humor lay in the fact that it was al-

ways well grounded, that it was always the standard-
bearer of truth or, at least, a majestic conviction of right
and of human sympathy, as much as the rest. For seventy
nights I heard his wit and colossal drollery convulsing
audiences, and never for one moment could hint that the
factor of license could seduce it. Mark Twain is never on
the platform the King's Jester; he is always the King.
(Applause.) I have seen him in sudden great junctures,—
you know I have seen you at times when you thought you
had imperilled for an instant this kingly quality, and the
thought always gave you exquisite pain. One night in a
certain Canadian City,[67] from time to time you could hear
thundering with regularity that reverberation of sound
from the audience, that always greeted him, and as we
drove back to our hotel Mark Twain was in a state of
mental misery because, forsooth, he had spent his share of
the whole talk merely spinning yarns, as he termed it, to
an audience which would next morning realize the means
he had sought to amuse them instead of giving them good
literature. But, as I reminded him, we would have the
same audience next night and he could give them as good
literature as the world had ever had. This he did, and the
result was as thunderingly flattering as before. Do you
remember, Mark, how we sang almost nightly that old
Mississippi ditty, "Jan and Dan"? I have never heard
who that particular Jan was, but it is enough for us all to
recognize here to-night that it was not and it is not yet
Mark.

Another of the things that I learned in that session
twenty-one years ago, was that along with that perfect
naturalness which was essentially his inherent character,
Mark Twain on the platform practised a painstaking

[art]. Do you remember, my old friend and big brother, that night in Buffalo when, after an excruciating succession of discharges of our shot, the steampipes began snapping and snorting, and you dared not answer them because you did not know how long they would keep up to the last word, and you went on with your reading while on your tongue all the time you had the request that "some one would please ask the janitor not to grit his teeth so loud"?

Another aspect of that artistic temperament is evidenced in this, that in all those seventy nights I never saw him betrayed into so much as [a] smile at himself, with the single exception when towards the close of a rather eventful evening, after the audience had been listening to his junior partner, the same audience broke into loud laughter on the appearance of the senior partner, and he could not help remarking, when a smile broke over his face, "Yes, that time they caught me." He confessed; he laughed, and I don't think his art left him even then, because I fancy it was the best art to laugh at the time. I saw in those days what an artist Mark Twain was, but Mr. Chairman, I am glad of the opportunity given me to confess in this gathering that I did not realize in those times how good a friend and how brotherly a well-wisher he was to me. Sometimes I think when the sevens of years have been seventy times seven, that confession is just what the world in general will make for itself. We have heard that the friend whom we celebrate has said he likes Cable well enough except for his religion. Well I am bound to declare the exception well taken. The longer I live the less I am satisfied with my religion myself. But for all that, I must say that from the depth of my religion—

Heaven send long years yet, Mark Twain, because you keep yourself too busy with more important matters. (Applause.)

Cable's fullest and most perceptive remarks on Mark Twain were made at the memorial service in New York on November 30, 1910.

Mr. Howells:[68]
If some finer and nobler novel than *The Grandissimes* has been written in this land, any time, I have not read it. From Mark Twain himself I learned to love the literature of the delightful Master who wrote that book, and it is with a peculiar sense of fitness in his presence here tonight that I ask you to join me in listening to George W. Cable.

Mr. Cable:
The great man whose memory tonight we give ourselves the tender joy to honor was one whom, I venture to say, no one who knew him personally and well ever thought of for a moment long enough to pass beyond a contemplation of the vast grotesqueness of his wit and humor without being impressed with the rare beauty of his mind.

I do not mean a beauty consisting in great structural symmetry or finish, as of some masterpiece of Greek or Gothic elaboration. I mean a beauty such as the illimitable haphazard of Nature a few times in our planet's history has hit upon, where angels would seem to have builded in a moment of careless sport, as in the Grand Cañon of the Colorado, or some equal wonder of supernal color and titanic form in that great West which had so much to do with the shaping of his genius—in so far as his genius was ever really shaped.

The beauty of that mind was a beauty of form and color, so to speak, rather than of mechanism. The marvelous union of crudeness and grace in those vast natural formations in the West symbolizes well the energy of his purposes, as the marvelous variety and intensity of their colors do the many passions of his spirit. Many, I say, for he was a packed cluster of passions. His passions for the charms of Nature compelled him to blindfold himself to them, as it were, whenever he would use his pen. Every one knows how he had to renounce the beautiful study lovingly built for him and furnished with every appointment for ease and convenience because of the enthralling views of hill, vale, and stream to be seen from its windows. As I repicture him in his housetop study at Hartford I see him sitting at a table where every time he lifted his eyes from pencil and paper they met only the blank stare of the wall against which it was set, and I remember one morning when, some time after he had started up to his work in that third-story room, I came upon him at a half-way stairlanding, gazing out of its window close into the vivid red and yellow depths of a maple steeped in autumn sunlight. Fastened to the spot he was, as he confessed himself in a burst of praise which I wish yet I had written down.

No less a passion was his feeling for humankind at large, and all his hot scoldings at it were only an outcome of elder-brotherly solicitude. On a certain evening some twenty-six years ago it was my fortune to be included with him in a very small group of men with whom he was particularly at ease—Osgood, Aldrich, O'Reilly—all now at rest. Dining with them in Boston, his unrestrained wit and titanic grimness of mirth kept them for hours wild with parrying cut and thrust, and literally beside themselves with jollity.[69] Yet that is but the background of the complete picture which is fresh in my memory to this day. Early next morning, as he and I left the city by train together, I was somehow emboldened to point out to him how the beauty of a sunrise on the river Charles was enhanced in poetic charm through the human interest given it by two or three especially slender and graceful factory chimneys distantly overtowering the flat land and low mists; and for half an hour it was my privilege to hear him set forth the poetry of toil with an eloquence so free from false sentiment, yet so reverential to all the affections and upward strivings of lowliest humanity, that I saw then what has never been hidden from me since—that he was made of a finer clay than the common type of men, if not the common type of great men.

It seems to me evident to all of us, if not to all the critical world, that that great human kindness of his was one of the foundations, the fundamental element, of his humor, and by it he gained the heart of the world. But I was warned in the first place that this was not to be an occasion for elaborate oratory, and that it would be better for us all if we should spend these moments as nearly as possible as if we sat at the fireside and talked of the friend who has lately gone from us to some other place to better his condition—whom we should some day rejoin. So I do not care how little coherence I shall have from this time on, through the few minutes I purpose occupying your time with a reminiscence or two of Mark Twain. These shall be in one or two cases at least to show, to illustrate, the reciprocation of this human kindness from the human race to Mark Twain in his goings and comings.

It was down in New Orleans that one day we were about sending him back up the Mississippi with Captain Bixby, his old captain, to complete his observations for the writing of his *Life on the Mississippi*. There was a great crowd around him to shake his hand. Men wished to shake his hand as they might have been glad to shake the hand of a king. It was in a worshipful spirit, in an affectionate spirit, that they crowded around, to have as they counted it that great privilege. And when we were all ordered off the boat, Osgood, who was with us, said that he had traveled through this country with Charles Dickens, that idol of his time in the hearts of all English-speaking readers, and that not even Charles Dickens had commanded the outward demonstration of affection which Mark Twain did at every turn, and which he received from every possible class and species of people. As we were going down on the narrow stagework that is characteristic of Mississippi steamboats, in a group of friends that included myself, we heard a man talking behind us, who I supposed must have represented and voiced the sentiments of hundreds who had spoken of Mark Twain in that way. This man said: "I have read every page he ever wrote, but I was so rattled and knocked to pieces with the opportunity when I came to shake his hand that I could not think of anything in the world to thank him for that he had written, except the *Heathen Chinee!*"

It is because of that hold he has on all our hearts—and I speak for the whole American people—it was that spirit that caused an audience once in Paris, Kentucky, who had applauded him until their palms were sore and until their feet were tired, and who had laughed as he came forward for the fourth alternation of our reading together—the one side of him dragging, one foot limping after the other —the peculiar way known to us all—the house burst into such a storm of laughter, coming from so crowded a house, that Mark Twain himself, grim controller of his emotions at all times, burst into laughter and had to acknowledge to me, as he came off the platform: "Yes, yes"—still laughing with joy of it himself—"yes; they got me off my feet that time."

I remember the hold he had upon children's hearts, another field of his human kindness to all humankind. It is illustrated in an experience he had in Cincinnati when certain children were brought by their aunt to hear Mark Twain read from his pages in that great city, brought down from the town of Hamilton, and who went back home in the late hours of the night, beside themselves with the delight of their clear understanding and full appreciation of his humor, saying to their kinswoman: "Oh, Auntie! Oh, Auntie! it was better than Buffalo Bill!"[70]

One point I should like to make to indicate the conscientiousness with which he held himself the custodian of the affections of the great mass of the people who loved him in every quarter of the land. It was the rigor of his art, an art which was able to carry the added burden beyond the burden of all other men's art, the burden of absolutely concealing itself and of making him appear, whenever he appeared, as slipshod in his mind as he was in his gait. We were at Toronto, Canada. The appointment was for us to read two nights in succession, and he had read one night. The vast hall was filled to overflowing. I heard from the retiring room the applause that followed every period of his utterance, heard it come rolling in and tumbling like the surf of the ocean. Well, at last, as we were driving home to our hotel, I found him in an absolutely wretched condition of mental depression, groaning and sighing, and all but weeping, and I asked him what in the world justified such a mood—a man who had just come from such a triumph. "Such a triumph?" he said. "A triumph of the moment; but those people are going home to their beds, glad to get there, and they will wake up in the morning ashamed of having laughed at my nonsense."

"Nonsense?" I said. "How is it nonsense?"

"I have spent the evening and their time, and taxed them to the best of their ability to show their appreciation of my wit and humor, and I have spent that whole time simply spinning yarns."

I said: "Don't mind; you are going to meet virtually the very same audience to-morrow, and to-morrow night you shall give them good literature, if any living writer in a living language has got that chance." I don't know if he slept that night, but I know he did what he did not often relish. He rehearsed, and rehearsed, and rehearsed, and the next night he gave them a programme which he chose to begin, at my suggestion, with the *Blue Jay's Message*. He left that house as happy as any one ever saw Mark Twain, and that was with a feeling of acute joy because he had won friends he considered worthy, he had won every handclap and applause with a programme worthy of honor.

One more point: every one knows that one of his passions was for history, and I assume that that passion for history was one of the demonstrations of his human kindness. It was the story of the human heart, and he loved history because it was the story of humanity.

One night we were in Rochester together. It was Saturday night, and for a wonder we were without an engagement that night, so we started out for a walk; we had gone a few steps when we found a bookstore, and at the same moment it was beginning to rain. I said: "Let us go in here." He said: "I remember I have not provided myself with anything to read all day to-morrow." I said: "We will get it here. I will look down that table, and you look down this." Presently I went over to him and said I had not found anything that I thought would interest him, and asked him if he had found anything. He said no, he had not; but there was a book he did not remember any previous acquaintance with. He asked me what that book was.

"Why," I said, "that is Sir Thomas Malory's *Morte d'Arthur*." And he said: "Shall we take it?" I said: "Yes; and you will never lay it down until you have read it from cover to cover." It was easy to make the prophecy, and, of course, it was fulfilled. He had read in it a day or two, when I saw come upon his cheekbones those vivid pink spots which every one who knew him intimately and closely knew meant that his mind was working with all its energies. I said to myself: "Ah, I think Sir Thomas Malory's *Morte d'Arthur* is going to bear fruit in the brain of Mark Twain." A year or two afterward, when he came to see me in my Northampton home, I asked him what he was engaged in, and he said he was writing a story of *A Yankee at the Court of King Arthur*. I said: "If that be so, then I claim for myself the godfathership of that

book." He said: "Yes; you are its godfather." I can claim
no higher honor than to have the honor to claim that here
and now, to-night, and to rejoice with you that we are
able to offer a tribute to our affection to the memory of
Mark Twain.

⊕ NOTES ⊕

[1] For a discussion of the "Drop Shot" column see my article "George Washington Cable's Literary Apprenticeship," *The Louisiana Historical Quarterly*, XXIV (Jan., 1941), pp. 168-186.

[2] Part of this letter is printed in L. L. C. Biklé, *George W. Cable: His Life and Letters* (New York, 1928), pp. 69-70.

[3] Chapters XLI-LI of *Life on the Mississippi* contain Mark Twain's account of his visit in New Orleans.

[4] This gathering was described in the New Orleans *Times-Democrat* of the day following. Mark Twain's stay in New Orleans was reported daily in the New Orleans newspapers, and those reports serve to fill in details between the lines of the account in *Life on the Mississippi*. See my article "Notes on Mark Twain in New Orleans," *The McNeese Review*, VI (1954), pp. 10-22.

[5] Cable's speeches on these two occasions are printed later in this volume.

[6] The letters in the Twain-Cable correspondence are included in Guy A. Cardwell, *Twins of Genius* (East Lansing, Michigan, 1953).

[7] *Mark Twain's Letters*, ed. Albert Bigelow Paine, I, (New York, 1917), pp. 426-427. For a remark of Cable's on this occasion see pp. 18 and 130 of the present volume.

[8] The story of Bras Coupé, an episode narrated in two chapters of *The Grandissimes*, tells of an African prince tragically broken in American slavery. Colossus is the servant of the backwoods preacher who is the title character in the short story "Posson Jone'." Joseph Frowenfeld and the Nancanou ladies are characters in *The Grandissimes*.

[9] *The Critic*, III, (March 24, 1883), pp. 130-131.

[10] To save space, phrases of salutation and conclusion have usually been omitted from the letters.

[11] Young daughter of Cable's widowed sister, Antoinette Cox. Portions of this letter and the one on April 5 are printed in Biklé, pp. 96-98.

[12] James R. Osgood had come from Boston; George E. Waring, Jr., from Newport; Richard Watson Gilder, Roswell Smith, and Lawrence Hutton from New York.

[13] See pp. 9-10 of this volume.

[14] Susan Coolidge was the pen name of Sarah Chauncy Woolsey (1835-1905), an author widely read in the 1880's.

[15] Major Kinney was an editor of the Hartford *Courant*.

[16] Charles Dudley Warner wrote "On Mr. Cable's Readings" for the *Century*, XXVI (June, 1883), pp. 311-312, and gave him unstinting praise for both his works and his reading of them, with the slight reservation that in the public reading he was not able to achieve "the subtle shading" which his private reading had. As Warner saw it, Cable's story "Posson Jone' " demonstrated, by its happy fusion of the two elements, that realism and idealism can join to produce fine art.

[17] Printed as a pamphlet by the Board of Administrators of the University (New Orleans, 1883).

[18] Published as "The Convict Lease System in the Southern States," *Century*, XXVII (Feb., 1884), pp. 582-599.

[19] See my article "Whittier Calls on George W. Cable," *New England Quarterly*, XXII (March, 1949), 92-96. Excerpts from letters Cable wrote home from Boston are printed in Biklé, pp. 109-113.

[20] Elizabeth Whiting's Boston letter in the New Orleans *Times-Democrat*, December 16, 1883.

[21] Yung Wing (Jung Hung) (1828-1912), the first Chinese graduate of an American university and a diligent worker for the education of Chinese in America, had married an American wife, a cousin of Mrs. Cable's, and lived in Hartford, where he had as friends Mark Twain, Twichell, and Charles Dudley Warner.

[22] Walter Cox, Cable's nephew, cultivated an interest in drawing as a boy and later made art his career.

[23] *Twins of Genius*, pp. 97-100. Excerpts from Cable's letters to his wife on January 28, 30, 31, February 13, 16, 18, appear in Biklé, pp. 116-119.

[24] At about this time Mark Twain was at work on the play *Colonel Sellers* and on dramatizations of *Tom Sawyer* and *The Prince and the Pauper*. It is not clear which play he completed during Cable's stay in his house or what new work he commenced.

[25] These lines open Longfellow's poem "The Hemlock Tree."

[26] *The Merry Adventures of Robin Hood of Great Renown, in Nottinghamshire* (New York, 1883).

[27] Gilder to Cable, July 25, 1884. This letter and others from Gilder are at Tulane University. One of Cable's letters to Gilder commenting in full on proposals Mark Twain had made for the multiple-author story has been printed in Harry R. Warfel, "George W. Cable

Amends a Mark Twain Plot," *American Literature,* VI (Nov., 1934), pp. 328-331.

²⁸ C. C. Buel was assistant editor of the *Century Magazine.*

²⁹ See Albert Bigelow Paine, *Mark Twain: A Biography* II, (New York, 1912), pp. 765-767.

³⁰ *The Critic,* V, (August 9, 1884), p. 66.

³¹ Quoted by Pond in a letter to Cable on June 18, 1884. Pond's letters to Cable are in the Cable Collection at Tulane University.

³² See E. F. Pabody, "Mark Twain's Ghost Story," *Minnesota History,* XVIII (March, 1937), pp. 28-35.

³³ See pp. 133-134 of this volume.

³⁴ In an article entitled "Creole Slave Songs" (*Century,* XXXI [April, 1886], pp. 807-828) Cable printed "Pov' Piti Momzel Zizi"; and in a companion article, "The Dance in Place Congo" (*Century,* XXXI [Feb., 1886], pp. 517-532) he included "Aurore Pradère."

³⁵ Apparently a member of the family of Frederick Theodore Frelinghuysen, Secretary of State in President Arthur's cabinet.

³⁶ See Paine, *Mark Twain,* II, p. 787; Mary Lawton, *A Lifetime with Mark Twain* (New York, 1925), pp. 78-79.

³⁷ Gerard E. Jensen, *The Life and Letters of Henry Cuyler Bunner,* (Durham, N. C., 1939), p. 77.

³⁸ Aurore Nancanou and her daughter Clotilde are characters in *The Grandissimes.* They are perhaps Cable's most successful portraits of the charming, mercurial Creole women.

³⁹ James Burrill Angell.

⁴⁰ Cable had read at the Opera House in Ann Arbor on March 10, 1884.

⁴¹ David Ross Locke.

⁴² Quoted in the *Critic,* V (Dec. 27, 1884), p. 308.

⁴³ In the Mark Twain memorial service held at New York on November 30, 1910, Cable referred to this incident. On the same occasion he told how at Paris, Kentucky, Mark Twain had laughed with his audience—something he did at no other time during their hundred appearances together. This speech is included in the present volume.

⁴⁴ *Mark Twain's Autobiography,* ed. Albert Bigelow Paine, I, (New York, 1924), pp. 91-92.

⁴⁵ This manuscript is in the Cable Collection at Tulane University. It is printed in full in my article "James Lampton: Mark Twain's Model for Colonel Sellers," *Modern Language Notes,* LXX (Dec., 1955), pp. 592-594.

⁴⁶ The article "New Orleans Before the Capture" had been prom-

ised for the *Century Magazine's* series on the Civil War written by participants, mainly commanders in the opposing forces. It appeared in the April issue.

[47] Owen Lovejoy (1811-1864) was a dedicated abolitionist who was prominent in Illinois politics and was elected to Congress in 1856.

[48] To a reporter for the St. Louis *Post-Dispatch* of January 9 Mark Twain gave a farcical account of his own actions when the train threatened to leave the track on the Mississippi River bridge. The interview is quoted in *Twins of Genius,* pp. 38-39.

[49] "New Orleans Before the Capture."

[50] Cable's weight was rarely as much as 111 pounds; at times it dropped below a hundred.

[51] Lucius Fairchild (1831-1896) was governor of Wisconsin 1866-1872.

[52] Cable's friend in New Orleans, Baron Ludwig von Reizenstein, had discovered a giant moth not previously known in North America and had named it Smerinthus Cablei. With Cable's assistance, Reizenstein published a report of his discovery in the *Century*, XXII (Oct., 1881), pp. 864-866.

[53] Thomas A. Hendricks was elected vice-president on the ticket with Cleveland in November, 1884.

[54] After Cable's essay appeared in January, the *Century* office had been deluged with letters opposing his views. It was decided not to make selections from them to publish in the magazine but rather to ask Henry W. Grady of the Atlanta *Constitution* to make what might be a composite statement for Cable's opponents in the matter. Grady's article, "In Plain Black and White," was in the April *Century;* Cable's reply to him, "The Silent South," was in the September issue.

[55] George Hoadly had been elected governor of Ohio in 1883.

[56] In an article on "Mark Twain in Oberlin," in the *Ohio State Archaeological and Historical Quarterly*, XLVII (Jan., 1938), pp. 69-73, Russell B. Nye cites the cool reception given Mark Twain's reading at Oberlin on this occasion to support the thesis that he later sought revenge by holding the town up to ridicule in his story "The Man That Corrupted Hadleyburg." Writing in the same periodical on "Mark Twain's Hadleyburg," LX (July, 1951), 257-264, Guy A. Cardwell argues convincingly that the satire in Mark Twain's story was aimed at no particular town.

[57] *Mark Twain, Business Man* (Boston, 1946), pp. 292-293.

[58] Pond to Cable, February 2, 1885 (at Tulane University).

[59] See *The Love Letters of Mark Twain* (New York, 1949), pp. 219-240.

[60] *Mark Twain's Letters*, II, p. 450.

[61] *The Love Letters of Mark Twain*, p. 231.

[62] *Mark Twain, Business Man*, p. 322.

[63] See Guy A. Cardwell, "Mark Twain's 'Row' with George Cable," *Modern Language Quarterly*, XIII (Dec., 1952), pp. 363-371; *Twins of Genius*, pp. 108-109; and my article, "Mark Twain, Cable, and a 'Professional Newspaper Liar,'" *New England Quarterly*, XXVIII (March, 1955), pp. 18-33.

[64] Baker to Cable, May 25, June 19, 1885 (at Tulane University).

[65] Letter of June 25, 1895 (at Tulane University). Excerpts from this letter are printed in *Twins of Genius*, p. 66, and L. L. C. Biklé, *George W. Cable: His Life and Letters*, p. 197 n.

[66] Cable's remarks on this occasion are quoted from "Mark Twain's 70th Birthday," *Harper's Weekly*, XLIX (Dec. 23, 1905), 1888-1889.

[67] Cable seems to have had in mind the readings at Toronto on December 8 and 9. For a retelling of this episode see pp. 133-134; also Paine, *Mark Twain*, II, 786. The doubt which Dixon Wecter expresses (*Mark Twain's Love Letters*, pp. 231-232) as to the genuineness of the episode is dispelled, surely, by the fact that in 1905 Cable recounted it in Mark Twain's presence.

[68] This speech was printed in the *Proceedings* of the American Academy and National Institute, III (1911), 21-24; and in the volume for 1922 of the "Academy Notes and Monographs" series, pp. 68-82.

[69] The reference is to the evening described in Mark Twain's letter to Howells on November 4, 1882, quoted on pages 9-10 of this volume.

[70] See Cable's letter to his wife on January 1, 1885, pp. 77-78 of this volume.